Systemic Leadership: Enriching the Meaning of our Work

Kathleen E. Allen
Cynthia Cherrey

American College Personnel Association and
National Association for Campus Activities

Copyright 2000 by
American College Personnel Association
And
National Association for Campus Activities

University Press of America, ® Inc.
4720 Boston Way
Lanham, Maryland 20706

12 Hid's Copse Rd.
Cumnor Hill, Oxford OX2 9JJ

Library of Congress Cataloging-in-Publication Data

Allen, Kathleen E.
Systemic leadership : enriching the meaning of our work / Kathleen E. Allen,
Cynthia Cherrey.
p. cm.
Includes bibliographical references and index.
1.   Leadership. 2. Organizational change. I. Cherrey, Cynthia. II. Title.
HD57.7.A42   2000   658.4'092—dc21   00-021890-CIP

ISBN 1-883485-19-3 (cloth: alk. ppr.)
ISBN 1-883485-20-7 (pbk: alk. ppr.)

⊖™The paper used in this publication meets the minimum
requirements of American National Standard for Information
Sciences—Permanence of Paper for Printed Library Materials,
ANSI Z39.48—1984

Dedications

Kathy would like to dedicate this book to her parents who have so generously given their love, support, and intellectual capacity, as well as modeled a deep care for others - all of which have helped her become who she is.

Cyn would like to dedicate this book to her family, who gives her the greatest gift of all - love. Ditto.

Table of Contents

Listing of Figures and Tables

Preface

Would the CEO of the Internet please stand up? Could we even identify a single person with the knowledge and power necessary to order a sudden or drastic change in what is quickly developing into one of the most powerful communication tools in the history of human civilization? There is no such person to be found. How does the Internet survive without job descriptions, strategic plans, or performance appraisals? The Internet, governed loosely by a broad range of persons, is a harbinger of institutions to come - sophisticated networks of people and resources that inherently cannot be "managed" using current models of leadership. While this could seem troubling to some traditionalists, it is an unavoidable reality that will need to be addressed by our institutions and also a rich and exciting opportunity for student affairs administrators to adapt to a dramatically new environment, and in the process help their students and institutions thrive!

The premise of this book is that all of us need to explore new ways of working that keep pace with the networked knowledge era. We believe that if we adopt a different perspective of our work and role in our organizations, the meaning of our work will be enhanced. In Part One of this book, we examine the subtle interplay of an emerging networked knowledge era and a receding hierarchical industrial era, beginning with an examination of how the former has been driven by an explosion of new communications technologies, global economic linkages, and a proliferation of information. From there, in Part Two, we explore the challenges posed by this new era, as well as solutions in the form of new ways of relating, influencing change, learning, and leading. In Part Three, we introduce a new approach to leadership—systemic leadership—which seamlessly integrates the four new ways of working, calls us to reframe our assumptions about working, and describes new roles for student affairs practitioners. We also introduce eleven individual and organizational capacities that will be needed to be effective in a networked knowledge world.

Over the long term, changing how we approach our work will be critical to our institutions' abilities to adapt and remain relevant. And while there is no short-term threat of extinction, there are significant benefits available to those persons and institutions that can bring these new mindsets and behaviors to their organizations. Our intention is to help transform higher education.

While we write with the perspective and background of student affairs leaders, we are confident that what we share in these pages has value for individuals from other sectors. A businessperson in Detroit, a public servant in Sacramento and a high school administrator in Miami face many common struggles and challenges because of the systematic shifts occurring throughout our society. The principles we have applied primarily to student affairs can apply equally well in many other contexts. Because the forces of change are affecting all of us, these new ways of relating, influencing change, learning, and leading are applicable to any kind of organization.

The information and observations that we have pulled together provide but a snapshot of our current thinking in our ongoing journey. Through our experiences at complex universities of radically different styles and sizes, research and reading across a range of disciplines, and efforts to inject creativity into time-honored tradition, we have come to this point in our thinking. This book offers our learning curve to individuals who want to create more effective organizations in today's environment. We have been able to practice and experiment with many of the ideas discussed in the coming pages, and have been able to enjoy some of the results. So far, a new systemic approach has helped us to more effectively influence positive change in our contexts, make sense of the challenging and confusing events in organizational life, and provided us with a set of useful, helpful concepts.

The writing process for this book has been truly collaborative. We each read widely in both different and similar disciplines. This has allowed us to leverage our individual knowledge into a shared intelligence. We thought through and created these concepts together—continuing to incorporate new ideas and practice along the way. In fact, one of our biggest challenges was to not reinvent the content of the book every time we met, based on the latest book or insight we had while implementing these ideas. We even wrote together—one of us at the computer and the other using pencil and paper to capture ideas—to help frame our thoughts. All in all, it was a wonderful generative process.

During our collaborative writing times, we often went for walks to discuss ideas and concepts. On one of our walks we came across a sculpture that embodied for us the current state of the concepts of this book. This spherical sculpture slowly rotates 360 degrees. As it turns, two birds with wings touching emerge as a pattern. Depending on one's point of view, the pattern is discernible, and at other points elusive. We believe that the concepts in this book are like this sculpture. The concepts paint a discernible whole and yet they leave space for others to contribute their own perspectives as well. It is up to the practitioners who read this book to create a whole cloth from these concepts. For us, the integration of practice with inquiry has brought these ideas to life. We invite the reader to do the same. In this new world, each of us has a role to play; each of us can look at our new societal context through a unique vantage point and experiment with new approaches that will help ourselves and those around us to thrive. This opportunity is not to be taken lightly, but is to be met with great energy and enthusiasm.

Acknowledgements

The paradox of acknowledgements is that it is impossible to be completely inclusive and appropriately brief. There are so many individuals who have helped to support and create this work, including scholars as well as practitioners. This has been a long journey with many people who have helped form our ideas over the years. However, that said, we would like to make the following attempt to acknowledge the influence that others have had on this work and ourselves.

We would like to thank the many colleagues who have attended our workshops and presentations - giving feedback and additional insights. We would like to acknowledge our many colleagues at the College of St. Benedict and the University of Southern California and other professionals for reading previous drafts. Special thanks goes to the administrative support we received from Phyllis, Regina, and Paul. Susan for her encouragement and the discovery of the great Maryland book sale. Rile for the sustenance in meals and support he has given us over the years when we wrote together. Larraine for her inspiration and the generous use of her north shore home. The National Association for Campus Activities (NACA) and The American College Personnel Association (ACPA) who have created a new alliance to support and disseminate this work. We offer a special thanks to those friends and family who have each in their own way helped these ideas be born and take life in the pages of this book. Your faith in us sustained us throughout our writing. Finally, this book is co-authored; we could not have done it without each other.

Part 1: Waves of Change

Chapter 1

The Dawning of the Networked Knowledge Era

"We have stepped into a future that we can't even see."
—Margaret Wheatley

Have you observed that the traditional strategies of creating change in your organization trigger more problems than they used to? Are decisions made outside the institution complicating your work more than in the past? Do you and your peers struggle to synthesize an overwhelming amount of data into practical knowledge?

These are all symptoms of living in a world of increased connectivity and the resulting challenges of working in a world of geometrically multiplying data. In this chapter, we will

- reflect on some of the implications these outside forces have on higher education,
- describe the significance of a new, "networked knowledge era",
- identify new ways of leading, relating, learning, and influencing change that can increase our effectiveness, and
- examine the reality of our work in relationship to the traditional expectations our organizations hold of student affairs practitioners.

Two major shifts occurring in the world are having a significant effect on how we work together, influence change and lead our organizations. The first shift is from a world of fragmentation to one of connectivity and integrated networks. The second shift is from an industrial to a knowledge era. Both shifts are fueled by the trend toward a global economy and by the increased use of technology and mass communications in our everyday lives.

From a Fragmented World to a Networked World

Characteristics of a Fragmented / Hierarchical World

A fragmented world is one where the parts of the system are primary and the understanding of the whole system is built from the parts (Capra, 1992; Kuh, Whitt, & Shedd, 1987; Wheatley, 1992). A machine, like a car, is built from various parts, using an assembly line to place the parts together. The whole car is created from various distinct parts. Each of the individual parts of a car is linked together in specific ways to ensure that a driver can control the speed and direction of the final result. The car (which is the whole) can be broken down to its parts and reassembled endlessly. If the ignition switch fails, the defective part is replaced and the car once again is fully operable. The same holds true with fuel pumps, batteries, or other aspects of the car. If we have a squeak or rattle, we take it to a mechanic, who initiates a diagnostic test designed to identify the defective part, which will then be replaced. The assumption behind the design of a car is that the whole is the sum of its parts.

Traditional hierarchies are good examples of such a fragmented worldview. Most hierarchical organizations create departments or divisions (independent parts) that have responsibility for specific functions (like a fuel pump, or ignition switch). The CEO, like the driver of a car, is expected to be able to control the speed and direction of the organization. The organization, like the car, has distinct boundaries from its outside environment (like the road in relation to the car) and yet it is designed to effectively access resources from the environment as well as contribute to it.

A fragmented worldview has a number of characteristics. First, *it views the organization from an "independent parts" perspective.* The assumption is that if something is not working, there is a part of the system that is defective and once it is replaced, it will allow the organization to once again function well. This focus on an organization's parts, leads to the erroneous conclusion that an organization is made up of the sum of its individual pieces. Hierarchical organizations and institutions of higher education often list their resources and assets in their year-end reports as evidence of their overall strength. This is a working example of the assumption that the whole organization is the sum of its tangible parts.

Second, such a worldview *works to maintain its boundaries from the outside environment as well as within itself.* For example, higher education operates as a hierarchy. The ivory tower image of the academy is an example of the reputation it has as being separate and bounded from the outside environment. The traditional boundaries between academic units and student affairs are an example of internal boundaries between parts.

Third, fragmented hierarchical organizations *use linear chains of causality to understand the dynamics of the system.* The linear chains of causality that exist in machines and assembly-line thinking influence this view of causality. It assumes that A causes B, which in turn causes C. We often spend time in our organizations sorting out the reason why something has occurred in order to prevent it from happening again. This activity is based in the assumption that these causal chains can be discovered and isolated.

Fourth, fragmented hierarchical organizations *tend to change incrementally.* New car designs usually evolve over time with each year having some new variations over the previous years. Hierarchical organizations also tend to change incrementally, and therefore are more stable and predictable from year to year. Higher education has a reputation for not radically changing its basic structure. Its seven-century history utilizing essentially the same original design attests to this.

Fifth, hierarchical organizations have a *simple complexity to them.* While these organizations are complex, the complexity can be understood if enough time and information is brought to bear on the problem. Usually the complexity is broken down into its component parts to be understood at that level before it is reassembled into a complex understanding. Simple complexity can still be broken down and understood when it is reassembled; however when problems become increasingly complex, they can no longer be understood by breaking them down into their parts.

Sixth, a fragmented hierarchical organization *assumes that it can be controlled from a key point in the system.* Like the driver in a car, the CEO is the individual who is perceived as being able to control the speed and direction of the organization. Many of the assumptions about change in higher education flow from this point; the phrase "change has to start at the top" is an example of the nature of change in hierarchical organizations.

As outlined in the above examples, the characteristics of a fragmented hierarchical structure are very familiar to those of us working within higher education. We have many examples that demonstrate that we live in hierarchies that operate from a fragmented orientation. We engage in incremental change, assert and defend our boundaries, participate in assumed linear causality, and are asked to control individual employees' and students' behaviors and organizational productivity. The dawning of a networked world does not supplant a hierarchical fragmented orientation; rather, it transcends it, adding another layer of dynamics and characteristics to the organizations within which we operate.

Characteristics of Networks

A networked world operates differently than one built on hierarchies and fragmentation. The Internet is a wonderful example of a network. It represents some of the paradoxes of networks, as well as some of the ways in which networks maintain order. The Internet has a basic structure within which individuals and organizations can create and operate. Its structure consists of nodes and links. Each node is a center for a web of connections and each of these nodes has web-like connections with other nodes. This structure is simple, and yet allows for great flexibility and evolution in the design and content of the World Wide Web. For example, individual actors can initiate change from anywhere within the system. A person can easily set up a new web site to become a part of the Internet or subscribe to an Internet service like America Online and have immediate access to topical chat rooms or initiate new topics of conversations. If we want to publish our thoughts or opinions, the Internet can facilitate the spread of those thoughts without going through traditional publishers or editorial review. New information spreads rapidly, but understanding and consolidating information into knowledge remains challenging. Search engines become another level of organizing information and sources of knowledge. Individuals can develop their own sorting vehicles for information and hence create their own meaning. The dynamics of the Internet are highly mobile. The jumps in usage can be non-linear. A web site can go from very few hits to 100,000 hits within a 24-hour period if its content is deemed attractive and interesting through the informal communication network of the web.

New web sites, individual actors, and content are constantly changing. Within this basic structure, the opportunities for individual initiative and creation are endless. In fact, the locus of intelligence in a network shifts to the active participants of the system (Negroponte, 1995). The active participants are the ones who shape the system, gradually and in an ongoing manner, based on their own knowledge and interests.

Networked organizations have different characteristics than fragmented hierarchical organizations. These characteristics do not replace hierarchical structures, but over time networks transcend the hierarchical processes and functions. While networks all have hierarchical aspects (for example search engines on the Internet provide a higher level of order than do web pages, or individual e-mail addresses), they bring a significant amount of linkage that traditional hierarchies do not have. Fragmented, parts-oriented hierarchies that protect their internal and external boundaries do not facilitate linkages. A networked world blurs organizational boundaries, creates connections, and influences the way we work.

A networked worldview has the following characteristics. First, *networks can only be understood from the perspective of the whole system* (Bennis, Parikh, & Lessen, 1994; Capra, 1996, 1992). Because networks are thick webs of intersecting connections, they cannot be understood by breaking them down into each individual connection. Instead, understanding of the system and its dynamics is visible only from a distance of time or space. Therefore, we metaphorically need to remove ourselves from the dance floor and go up to the balcony in order to see the dynamics of the web of activity. Networked systems are always more than the sum of their parts. If we de-constructed the Internet, we would find a series of electronic connections and nodes. In addition, most of these connections and linkages would be intangible to the eye because they are made up of electronic bits. They would not reflect tangible parts with distinct boundaries like the parts of a car. When these electronic connections come together within an operating structure, they synergistically emerge into the entity we call the Internet. The Internet is more than the sum of its individual parts and can only be understood from a systems perspective. Human groups and organizations operate in a similar way. When five members of a basketball team work together and transcend their individual skills, we know that an effective team has been developed. This team is the synergistic result of the unique composition of each member as well as their ability to work together and heighten each other's play.

Second, due to their high degree of connectivity, *networks create blurred boundaries in organizations*. Links and connections span traditional boundaries and make it impossible to have distinct boundaries the way various machine parts do in a car. In recent years, the traditional boundaries of higher education have eroded. Community service, increased internships, and parental involvement as well as political, social, and economic issues have penetrated the academy challenging us to reconsider research, teaching, curricular and co-curricular balance, type and quality of services, and academic majors.

Third, *networks behave in non-linear ways*. Unlike the linear causality of machines, the vast number of connections creates opportunities for discontinuous change within organizations (Handy, 1989). Discontinuous/non-linear jumps make single causality fundamentally useless. The reason for this is that the connectivity of the system allows for many variables from both near and far to create ripple effects that affect the whole system. Non-linear logic teaches that "it is only by proceeding deductively—by working backward from the outcome—that you can manage the storm of variables that will assault any business strategy" (Taylor, & Wacker, 1997, p.10).

Fourth, *networks are always in dynamic flux*. When many highly connected variables are in play, high speeds and high degrees of movement become natural characteristics of the system. We experience this movement in the way problems seem to mutate, the increase in the number of novel problems that appear each year, and the diminishing of the rules that used to give us a sense of predictability. As the number of variables in the system increases, we experience an accelerating sense of speed. This experience of speed is a symptom of the frequency of movement within the system. In fact we have all gone through a real and felt collapse of time with the onset of networked computer systems, e-mail, voice mail, cellular phones, and fax machines on our campuses. As the number of ways people have to reach us increases, we experience an increase in the requests for a response, which in turn causes us to feel like we are living in a rapidly changing world.

Fifth, *network systems have complex complexity*. In contrast with simple complexity, complex complexity geometrically compounds the variables and unknowns we need to work with for strategic planning and decision-making. A networked system is never closed from outside influences, and is therefore always affected by variables that exist outside our own departments or higher education as a whole. This makes it impossible to research everything or understand completely all the variables when we make decisions or solve problems. Our traditional mindset suggests that with persistence and good information, we will be able to gather all the knowledge we need to make a good decision. Complex complexity means we will need to become comfortable with ambiguity (Clark, 1985). There will always be an element of continual learning and missing information in our decision-making or problem analysis—it is a characteristic of a networked system (Vaill, 1996).

Sixth, *networks can be influenced but they cannot be controlled*. In a 1998 obituary for Internet pioneer Jon Postel, the Financial Times noted that Postel helped influence the development of the Internet realizing that no single person or entity could "control" it:

> *"The Internet works because computer scientists all over the world are prepared to reach agreement on the best standards to adopt. The process of reaching that agreement is managed by a relatively small number of people, of whom Postel was one. Their power stems not from official status or governmental nomination, but from their ability to create a consensus"* (p. 20).

The consensus, in turn, stems from a shared purpose. Were one person to try to force his or her will on the overall Internet—even a giant such as a Bill Gates—he or she would surely fail. Due to the dynamic movement and high degree of connectivity, networks do not respond to force—in fact they naturally resist it. Wet sand is composed of silicone and saline and performs in a way similar to a network. It resists the imprint of our foot when we slap our foot down on the wet sand; however, when we place our foot on it and wait, the wet sand allows our foot to sink into it. This capacity to make an imprint by "placing and waiting" is like the influencing strategies we use in groups. Many student affairs staff members have been called upon to influence residence hall cultures or do crowd control at a major event. We know from experience that influencing works much better than force. The same is true of networks. The more people we have who are intentionally nudging a networked system in the same direction, the more we can influence the direction of the network.

These characteristics of networks have become increasingly more familiar to student affairs practitioners. Over the last decade, we have felt the increasing rapidity of change and the lessening effectiveness of control strategies. We have experienced more people who have opinions about how we do our jobs. In addition, we are affected by the blurred boundaries between our divisions and the outside community. Global, economic, political, and societal issues affect our campus and our students and the dynamics on campus. Effective staff members are beginning to behave differently. It used to be that effectiveness was measured in part by a person's ability to be autonomous and protect his or her boundaries. Now, effectiveness is dependent on a person's ability to develop and maintain cross boundary relationships and see the whole system, not just his or her own part. New rules have replaced old rules. The old rule that said "everything will become clear when I grow up" has been replaced by the need for constant learning and letting go of old ways of doing things.

Over time, higher educational institutions have been adjusting to the incorporation of networked dynamics into our traditional hierarchies. However, because we have not named the differences between how fragmented hierarchies and connected networks operate, we often find ourselves caught between old practices and evolving standards of professional effectiveness. Sometimes, we use hierarchical strategies when networks would be more effective and vice versa. Student affairs practitioners have many insights and capacities to offer networked organizations because we have been practicing influencing a student culture, which operates more like a network than a hierarchy. The summary of the characteristics of fragmented hierarchies and connected networks is listed in Table 1.

Characteristics of Hierarchies and Networks

Fragmented/Hierarchical Orientation	Networked Orientation
Parts perspective	Whole system perspective
Distinct boundaries	Blurred boundaries
Linear causality	Non-linear causality
Change incrementally	Dynamic flux
Simple complexity	Complex complexity
Can be controlled	Can be influenced

Table 1.1

New Ways of Relating and Influencing Change

Networked organizations require us to develop and practice two new ways of working. The first is **new ways of relating**. *New ways of relating involves the capacity to build and maintain effective cooperative relationships across the boundaries of an organization and between the organization and the community.* In a networked world, one's value is measured by one's connection to it. Our relationships need to model and keep pace with the nature of the system. If the system is full of connections, then we need to be in connection as well. *New ways of relating also involves the need to think relationally.* Since networks have many variables in play, and linear causality does not work in open systems, a new way of thinking is needed. This new way of thinking involves learning how different variables relate to and affect each other. Relational thinking is similar to thinking systemically. Not only must we see the whole instead of one part, we must also develop the capacity to understand how variables will affect each other over time. *New* *ways of relating also involves the development of emotional intelligence on both individual and group levels* (Goleman, 1995, 1998). Emotional intelligence requires developing a personal emotional competence in the areas of self-awareness, self-regulation, and motivation. It also encompasses social emotional competence including empathy and social skills. The reason why emotional intelligence becomes more important in a networked world is that the flow of emotions as well as information is increased within a networked system. If the members of a networked organization have low emotional intelligence, rumor, fear, and amplification of all emotions will occur. This results in an organizational drain of energy and resources as staff members respond to the emotional content of communications instead of the informational content.

Networked organizations also require us to develop and practice **new ways of influencing change.** *New ways of influencing change involves more organic strategies that take into account the non-linear dynamics of the connected systems and its response to force.* Networks resist force but hierarchies traditionally use force and power to move people. If we continue to use traditional change strategies in a networked world, we can hinder our success. *New ways of influencing change also involves developing an understanding of how the dynamics of a network operate and where the key points of leverage are within the system.* When we learn to spot these points of influence, we can use the dynamics of the system to bring it to health.

From an Industrial to a Knowledge Era

At the same time our world has become more interconnected, there has been another movement from the industrial age to the post-industrial age—also called a knowledge era. In the 1950s the shift in value from capital to knowledge began (de Geus, 1997). As the external environment became more turbulent and less controllable, an organization's ability to cope with a changing world became more important. Therefore, the development of the capability of shifting and changing became more critical as did the development of new skills and attitudes toward organizational learning. It was at this point that the shift from an industrial worldview to a knowledge era occurred. Depending on the field, this shift has been occurring since the 1950s. For example, in the 1980s, growing external turbulence challenged the health care field. Some believe that the institution of higher education now and in the future will experience greater and greater external turbulence (Duderstadt, 1995, 1997).

Characteristics of an Industrial World

In an industrial age, we organized processes around the production of material products in an assembly-line mode, and we used machines to extend our physical powers (Banathy, 1993). There are five characteristics that describe how knowledge and information were used in an industrial age. These characteristics each reflect and are influenced by the assembly line, fragmented, and hierarchical thinking embedded in an industrial worldview.

First, *all resources are seen as finite* in an industrial worldview. In an industrial world, labor, capital, and natural resources are considered the primary sources of organizational wealth. The more access an organization has to these resources, the more competitive it is. In the industrial age, knowledge and information are not consciously thought of as resources in an organization. Each of these industrial primary sources has a finite quality and assumes the rules of a zero-sum game. If one organization has more capital than its competitor, it is seen as more successful. Organizations protect whatever resource is most valuable to them. For example, if they see labor as cheap and capital as essential, then in times of economic downturns, the work force would be cut in order to ensure the company thrived.

Second, *the amount of information available is perceived as knowable.* Information overload was not experienced as an issue because there was not as much of it. In the 1950s and 1960s, home encyclopedias were popular. The assumption was that they contained all the information a child needed to write a report. Today, the idea that there would be a condensed single source of information and knowledge is inconceivable, due in part to the ongoing development of new information and generation of data. Information and data were also given an almost "magical" quality. Because so much was unknown, any information was therefore seen as relevant. This led managers to believe that data and information were synonymous with knowledge.

Third, *information in an industrial era is seen as controllable.* Both the direction and flow of information is managed. Positional managers know more than line workers; information is withheld rather than shared. The belief that information can be managed and the distribution can be controlled is based in a hierarchical worldview. In an odd way, many faculty members reinforce this industrial era view by controlling the direction and flow of information in the classroom. This expectation is placed on them by the institutional culture of higher education, which in turn has been influenced by the industrial era.

Fourth, *information and knowledge are applied in specific situations.* In an industrial era, when a part of the organization is not working, key experts were sought out and asked to study the problem. Research and knowledge are applied in specific situations and are utilitarian in nature. There is a familiar analog to this use of knowledge in higher education institutions. Our institutions are designed to break down knowledge by courses.

Fifth, *learning is sequential and task specific.* In an industrial era, learning occurs first and application afterward. When what we have learned in school is insufficient, additional training is provided. However, the additional training is task specific rather than general. There is an echo of this kind of thinking in the way higher educational institutions structure their learning. While some majors welcome the integration of experience, skills and concepts, others resist bringing theory into relationship with real life applications. This is a way we reinforce the ideas behind sequential learning.

In an industrial world, ideas like capital assets, mass production, and economies of scale also form the basis for how an organization does things. In higher education, we built universities based on these principles. Labor and capital in the form of tuition revenue and endowment are considered our primary resources. We think of the production of knowledge as one of our products, measured in part by the number of publications our faculty have. The prerequisites, general curriculum, and major requirements set up for our students have an eerie resemblance to an assembly line. Needless to say, most of our institutions of higher education fit right into the industrial era. This should not surprise us; many institutions were created and designed within this era. However, what if we are challenged to radically change the basic assumptions of operating from an industrial model to a knowledge worldview?

There are two good reasons to consider this possibility likely. First, we are experiencing greater outside turbulence, which is creating more need for higher education to embrace the challenge of change (Ikenberry, 1996). Some indications that higher education is responding to these challenges include

• growing tensions around learning versus instruction paradigms,
• experimentation in the way we structure our organizations—distance learning versus residential colleges, etc.,
• discussions on how we develop and sustain teaching and research-bounded disciplines versus blurred boundaries between traditional

disciplines, and collaborative versus individual research, and
• debates about our role within society—production of knowledge versus the need to develop citizen leaders, liberal arts vs. vocational preparation, "diversity" versus "excellence," etc.

The second reason we may feel the need to consider shifting from an industrial frame of operating to a knowledge era is that our students will be knowledge workers. In order to prepare them for the 21st Century, we need to develop their capacity to learn individually and organizationally as well as their ability to think systemically. This will require a shift in how we currently structure our organizations and the pedagogy we use to facilitate learning.

Characteristics of a Knowledge-Based World

An increasing connectivity and networking within the world in which we live mark the advent of a knowledge era. As mass communications, the global economy, and computer technology create ever-expanding webs of connections, a series of second-, third-, and fourth-order implications are created. This is called the spiral effect of connectivity. As connectivity is increased, it feeds dynamic movement within a system. This accelerating movement is the result of radically increasing the number of variables that can affect the dynamics of the system. This dynamic movement in turn increases the amount of complex complexity within the system. Again, as connectivity increases the number of variables and movement within a system, it becomes increasingly difficult to fully understand the system. This in turn increases the need for continual learning on both individual and organizational levels. The need for leveraging individual intelligence into shared organizational intelligence is necessary for the organization to continue to adapt and thrive within a constantly changing turbulent environment. In fact, the organization that can learn faster and apply this organizational learning to the way it operates will maintain a competitive advantage (de Geus, 1997).

The Spiral of Connectivity

• Connectivity feeds dynamic movement,
• which feeds complexity,
• which feeds the need for learning on both an individual and organizational level,
• which is necessary in order for the organization to continually evolve and thrive within the turbulent environment, and
• which requires greater connectivity.

The general characteristics of a knowledge era include the explosion of information and knowledge, accelerating advancements in intellectual technology, new modes of communication, extension of our cognitive powers, and a resulting new world view that includes systems thinking and leveraging intellectual capital within an organization (Banathy, 1993). There are five characteristics that capture the shift in the value and use of information in a knowledge era.

The first is that the key resource of our organization—*knowledge—is infinite* instead of finite. This creates a fundamental shift from the industrial age where primary resources were finite. In an industrial age, scarcity of resources led to competition as a primary way of operating. Knowledge, however, is increased when it is shared. In fact, when knowledge is withheld it actually hinders an organization's ability to learn. In a knowledge era, cooperation becomes economically efficient because learning is accelerated through sharing and innovation is increased through collaboration (Halal, 1998).

The Linux operating system is a good example of this principle in action. Linux is an open source program similar to Microsoft Windows. It has been distributed for free on the Internet with an invitation to individuals to play with it and give feedback. In August 1999, a competition was held between Linux and Microsoft. Hackers were invited to attempt to crash the two systems. In the first day, Microsoft Windows crashed nine times while Linux continued to run. The supposition was that Linux benefited from the ongoing upgrading of their system due to the sharing of knowledge and learning from the diversity of users.

Second, in a knowledge era, *the increase in the amount of information is accelerating.* The amount of information and data in the world has been doubling with increasing speed over the last century. In 1990, it was estimated that all the data in the world was doubling every eighteen months (Russell, 1998). This increasing speed leads to very different challenges for organizations as they attempt to transform data and information into usable knowledge (Allen, Stelzner, & Wielkiewicz, 1998). Due to the amount of information in the system, there is a growing amount of misinformation as well. Sorting out what is relevant information for decision making and planning is much more complex now than 20 years ago. Our faculty and administrative staff struggle with this reality. Keeping up with our fields and finding ways to synthesize advances into our classroom becomes a growing challenge.

Third, there are *expanding vehicles by which information flows through and into organizations* in a knowledge era. Mass communications and computer technology have increased the number and kinds of ways information and opinions can be spread. Where ideas used to be screened by publishers, newspapers, or managers, now anyone can distribute ideas or complaints through the Internet or even design a press release. The number of disclosures of behind the scenes behaviors by CEOs of major corporations supports the shift to a culture where nothing remains private. As we see a continued increase in these vehicles by which information flows freely, information sharing also becomes more natural than information withholding.

Fourth, in a knowledge era, *systemic knowledge is more valued and critical*. Explanatory power occurs on the systemic level not in its smaller parts. Therefore, thinking holistically instead of compartmentally becomes an essential skill. Higher education has a significant challenge if we want to teach students to think systemically because our structure actually diminishes the opportunities we have to teach systemic thinking. For example, the amount of interdisciplinary teaching being done on our campuses is not as great as many faculty would like because the curriculum and resource allocation are not structured to support it.

Fifth, *ongoing learning for both individuals and organizations is crucial*. Given the dynamic nature of networks, learning never becomes a terminal or sequential process. The continued integration of concepts, capacities, and practice becomes the way individuals and organizations reflect on and process insights in order to transform information into knowledge and wisdom.

The summary of the characteristics of an industrial and knowledge era are in Table 1.2.

Characteristics of an Industrial and Knowledge Era

Industrial Era	Knowledge Era
Primary resources include labor, capital, and material resources and are finite in nature	Knowledge is the primary resource and is infinite in nature
Needed information is knowable	Accelerating amount of information leads to information overload and misinformation
The flow and direction of information is controllable, leading to information withholding	Expanding vehicles spread information, leading to information sharing
Contained application of information	Systemic knowledge
Learning is sequential and task specific	Ongoing learning and integration of knowledge needed on both an individual and organizational level

Table 1.2

These knowledge era ideas and behaviors are not currently modeled widely within institutions of higher education. Much of the pedagogy in use reinforces individual generation of knowledge based on a competitive model. This teaches individuals how to withhold information rather than learn cooperatively. While the cooperative learning pedagogy may be an important teaching trend because it complements the dynamics of a knowledge era, it is still not widely accepted. In a world where collective and shared learning will be a valuable asset to an organization, higher education is not adequately preparing students to contribute.

There are signs of hope, however. Many co-curricular and residential environments are designed to support the development of community learning, not just individual learning. When student affairs practitioners help a student organization learn to function more effectively as a group, they are teaching the skill of shared learning that students will need in the future.

New Ways of Learning

Just as a networked world requires new ways of relating and influencing change, the knowledge era is triggering a third new approach to work—**new ways of learning**. New ways of learning involve *leveraging diverse perspectives into collective or shared group intelligence and integrating theory, new capacities, and practice with one another* (Senge, 1996). Theories and concepts hold new information that helps people intellectually understand a subject or phenomenon. Capacity building helps individuals develop skills and abilities they need to apply theory and concepts—something of far more lasting benefit than the simple memorization of traditional instruction. Practice opportunities are needed to give individuals time to integrate theory and capacities in order to accomplish a task or activity. When children learn to play the piano, they integrate theory, capacity and practice. Their music teacher helps them learn to read music and understand the theory behind music. The teacher also helps piano students to learn the skills to play. Many of us remember learning the scales before we could move onto a melody. Finally, all piano students have to practice, practice, and practice. The practice piece of learning to play the piano is needed to integrate the theory and skills.

In higher education, the faculty help students develop concepts and theory, while student affairs help students develop capacities and create opportunities to practice the integration of learning. The current problem within higher education is the fragmentation of the learning process. If we want to accelerate new ways of learning, we would develop ways for dialogue and sharing of insights between faculty, student affairs staff, and students with the intention of integrating and creating new shared knowledge about the learning process.

The Reality of Our Work: Organic Realities and Mechanistic Expectations

The industrial age has subtly shaped the mechanistic assumptions upon which we base our work. As we began to develop machines that extended the reach of our body—like the car extended our legs—we also began to think in more machine-like ways and apply these mechanistic principles to our work, our organizations, and ourselves. Most of our organizations continue to have mechanistic images. It is the authors' belief that organic images fit with the dynamic change embedded in a networked world—in fact, one could measure the movement toward networked organizations by the metaphors in use at work.

Which reality is currently in place in organizations—networks or fragmented hierarchies? The tendency is to answer this question from an either-or perspective; in reality, the answer is more likely that both the organic/networked reality and mechanistic/fragmented expectations co-exist. Many of us have images of how our organizations ought to work. The networked organizations function more organically and hierarchical organizations are based on machine-like images. The expectations of a machine bring to mind the criteria by which we judge our car, in part, by its dependability, predictability, and efficient use of fuel. With these mechanistic images, it is very easy to begin to judge our organizations and our behavior from standards that have been developed for evaluating machines. Taylor (1915) contributed to this connection with his time motion studies in factories across the country. Skinner (1953) reinforced this assumption through his experiments using rewards and punishments to control behavior in the laboratory with rats. It is fascinating that Skinner's concepts were applied so widely in organizations, as it reinforced the belief that human beings were actually programmable. We need to name the conflicts these mechanistic assumptions create in organizations that increasingly function in organic ways.

Informed Experimentation and Perfection

If we trace our assumptions through observing organizational behavior, we believe we can always be right the first time. This assumption implies we can think of an idea and if we plan it out carefully enough, it will be perfect the first time we implement it. This is "the way things ought to be"—however, "the way things are" looks quite different. The way things actually occur is: we come up with an idea, plan, and implement the idea the best we can. The first time we implement the program or try out a new idea, it looks more like informed experimentation. In reality, there are always things that we underestimate, factors we do not consider, or surprises that occur. Each time we try something new, we learn from our experience and use that learning to problem-solve and refine the original idea. Even though we intellectually understand the difference between perfection the first time and the reality of experimentation, we often measure others and ourselves by the standard of perfection. This is one of the fundamental differences between the way we think things ought to be and the way things actually are.

Core Values and Goals

Another juxtaposition of "the way things ought to be" and "the way things are" is imbedded in the process of developing goals. Each year staff members write out goals and objectives for the following year. Often, the performance appraisal process is tied to the accomplishment of these goals and objectives. Sometimes, quarterly conversations occur with supervisors to provide updates and progress reports. That's the way things ought to be; however, the way things actually are is that surprising challenges show up in the fall, winter, or spring that become more important than some of the goals we identified earlier. This poses a dilemma. We need to shift our focus to these new goals while the system measures our performance on goals developed months earlier. The way things ought to be implies that we can predict, with complete certainty, what will be important for the next 14 months. However, the reality of the way things are suggests there will always be times when additional or new goals will take priority over original goals. When this occurs, we need to adjust our time and focus to meet these new challenges or problems. If we ignored these new issues, we would not be serving the organization. The reality in goal setting is that the dynamic flux of a networked world creates situations that are more fluid than our goal setting system would have us believe.

Control is Rare and Control is Expected

Another hierarchical assumption that organizations operate under is that control is possible and even expected. Management literature implies that managers should be able to control all the employees that report to them. This form of control is necessary in order for the manager to deliver the expected outcome or product. Managers are given authority and power over employees in order to ensure control. This is how the system is designed and how it ought to operate. However, when dealing with human beings, absolute control is rare and some might say impossible to achieve. Just consider the infinite number of ways people can resist control when they put their minds to it. While the illusion of control may exist for a period of time, it cannot be maintained over the long-term. In institutions where new forms of organization are being experimented with, control as we traditionally know it is rare.

Innovation and Efficiency

Another juxtaposition is embedded in the value we place on efficiency. In the hierarchical images of the way things ought to be, efficiency is the standard of competence. We measure the effectiveness, in part, by how fast we get from one point to another. We moan about going to committee meetings because they rarely live up to our standards of efficiency. We even use efficiency as a way of measuring competence. We are most competent when everything goes "right" and no "humanness," such as emotions, interferes with our goal. The reality in human organizations is very different. Human organizations are not efficient. At meetings we watch the same conversation come up again and again, knowing that redundancy, while frustrating, is normal. Human beings are great at innovation, creativity, and effectiveness but do not accomplish anything in the most efficient way.

Probability and Predictability

Another assumption we have is about predictability. We believe people's behavior ought to be predictable in organizations. The way things are demonstrates that we rarely have this sense of predictability (Clark, 1985). We can see patterns that may indicate the probability of a future event, but we cannot predict minutely what is actually going to happen. This is similar to weather systems. We can accurately predict the weather today but not a week from now. There are too many intervening variables to ensure predictability even three to five days from today. While general weather patterns give us some indication of what future weather will be like, these patterns do not tell us specifically what will happen on any given day. Weather is like the human dynamics in organizations; there is very little predictability beyond the immediate time frame. Our organizational assumption is that events ought to be predictable and we spend many hours trying to actually predict events. However, the reality is that predictability is rare.

Which reality matches real-life experience? Do organizations get things right the first time? Are people and events in organizations controllable? Is everything efficient? Do the goals we identify in the spring actually reflect the goals that are most important the following year? Is predictability the norm? Or do organizations exhibit informed experimentation? Do important goals show up in the fall that could not have been anticipated? Is control more of a rarity than the norm? Are organizations effective but not necessarily efficient? Do we understand what is ahead of us through patterns of evidence and realize that complete predictability is impossible? If an organization operates more like "the way things ought to be," it reflects the characteristics of a fragmented, industrial and hierarchical paradigm. However, if organic realities actually reflect an organization's way of working, then it is being affected by the characteristics of a networked knowledge era. Most likely, we are living in a world that reflects both the mechanistic and organic realities. Table 1.3 summarizes the differences between "the way things ought to be" and "the way things actually are" in organizations.

Competing Expectations and Realities

The way things ought to be	The way things actually are
Perfection is expected the first time	Informed experimentation
Goals are predictable with complete certainty	Additional and new goals will always appear
Control is expected	Absolute control is rare and cannot be maintained over the long term
Efficiency is the standard of competence	Redundance and detours fuel creativity and innovation
Predictability is assumed	Probabilities are the norm

Table 1.3

If organizations are more like the ways things are instead of the way things ought to be, we are living in a networked system—in organizations that have more of an organic nature than a mechanistic one. Once we accept the organic nature of organizations, we can let go of judging ourselves as deficient each time organizations behave naturally. We can begin to look at how things naturally occur, and use that knowledge to lead and design organizations that complement the strengths and dynamics of human systems. Networks are creating another organizational culture within hierarchical organizations. In the future, the networked culture may transcend the hierarchical culture; however, in the meantime, our world will have conflicting expectations and realities—signs we currently are living in both worlds.

Living in Both Worlds

The paradigm of a fragmented, hierarchical world is of one truth, one single answer, one best way. Taylor (1915) in his scientific management theory wrote there is always one best strategy. It is a paradigm of either-or logic. Its roots are in Aristotlian logic, which argues that a statement is either "true or false" and Newtonian science, which argues that physical systems are linear. Either-or logic is a part of the traditional paradigm in which we grew up.

There are times in our present work when the traditional mindset and way of working is advantageous. Yet, in this networked knowledge era, there is a significant downside to using only this method. The new ways of relating, influencing change, learning and leading described in this book do not supersede the traditional paradigm, nor make it right or wrong—or less valuable. It is just that the traditional paradigm is valid for a narrowing range of experiences.

The two paradigms are not mutually exclusive. You do not choose between them, selecting one and rejecting the other. Instead, our back-pack of resources should include competencies for both. However, since the networked world is new and unfamiliar territory, this book focuses on the capacities needed to be effective in the emerging paradigm. Practicing systemic leadership means assessing the worth of operating from a tradi-tional view and the emergent view, given the context, and choosing accordingly. Systemic leadership is "both-and" not "either-or."

Implications for Higher Education—Change to Thrive

It is clear that current institutions are poorly prepared to operate within a networked knowledge era. Many institutions are designed to operate as fragmented and hierarchical organizations. Further, we have struc-tured teaching on industrial age principles, putting us increasingly out of sync with the world around us. As the world becomes more and more connected and knowledge based, higher education will be challenged to develop students who can effectively contribute to this world. This will be difficult to do unless all of us are willing to transform organizations and ourselves in a way that supports the development of connections among us and facilitates the learning we need to do individually and organizationally to accomplish transformation.

New Ways of Leading

New ways of relating and influencing change are needed to respond to the increasingly networked world in which we live. The knowledge era, in turn, triggers the need for new ways of learning. These three new ways of working synergistically combine to form **new ways of leading**, developed on the principles that flow from a networked knowledge era. Such leadership strategies need to *incorporate the systemic dynamics of an organization.* New ways of leading also need to *facilitate the devel-opment of shared learning, influence change in different ways, relate ideas and people in ways that cross boundaries, and use new forms of cohesion that help organizations retain direction and coherence without control.* When we shift our paradigm from fragmented, hierarchical and industrial thinking to networked knowledge assumptions, we can dis-cern simpler and more effective ways of accomplishing goals.

New Roles for Student Affairs Practitioners

Student affairs practitioners have many capacities and insights to help organizations transform themselves into networked knowledge era organizations (Allen & Cherrey, 1994). Relating is a key strength of the profession because we have so many opportunities to practice bringing people together in effective collaborations. Student affairs practitioners also have practice in the organic ways of influencing change. For example, our experience in planting seeds in the student culture in order to facilitate individual development is an organic change strategy. We also have experience helping students integrate their learning experiences especially in relation to developing the whole person. While these are good starting places, student affairs practitioners will also have to let go of the constraining beliefs they have about their capacity to influence institutional change. As practitioners in the world of academe, we often see ourselves as being on the margin, as being powerless. Instead we need to recognize that we can either choose to remain passive or to influence the needed change in our institutions. Given the shift from a fragmented industrial world to one that is networked and knowledge based, the capacities of student affairs practitioners are critical to institutions' abilities to meet the challenges and demands for change in higher education (Cherrey & Isgar, 1998). These institutional needs require that student affairs professionals bring their talents to the table, make necessary changes in their practice, develop new capacities, challenge traditional ways of working and develop the new relationships needed to influence institutional leadership and transformation. To do so, we need to develop new ways of relating, influencing change, learning, and leading. Part Two describes in greater detail these four new ways of working to face the challenges presented by living in a networked knowledge era. Finally, in Part Three, we identify the roles and capacities needed to be effective in this changing world.

Higher education can and needs to make a difference in our society. Student affairs practitioners have a responsibility to help institutions respond to the challenges facing higher education. Our students will impact the world in greater proportion than their numbers. Higher education needs to fulfill its promise to these students and society and prepare students to live and work in a networked, knowledge-based world. Our students learn in part by watching what we do as individuals and institutions. If we are to prepare students for the 21st Century, we must work to transform our institutions and ourselves. The time for student affairs to take a significant role in institutional leadership is now.

Reflective Questions:

1. What are the implications these ideas have on the structure of student affairs divisions?
2. What are the implications these ideas have on the structure of higher education?
3. What implications do these ideas have for how we communicate across boundaries?
4. What are some encouraging signs that institutions are changing?
5. What are the challenging issues that must be faced if we are to transform higher education?
6. Is there a unique and important role for colleges and universities in preparing students for leadership and work in a networked knowledge era?

Part 2: New Ways of Working

Chapter 2

New Ways of Relating

"Everything participates in the creation and evolution of its neighbors. There are no unaffected outsiders. No one system dictates conditions to another. All participate together in creating the conditions of their interdependence."

—Wheatley & Kellner-Rogers

A polyamide resin and an epoxy resin are two different molecular compounds that, when united become powerful epoxy glue. As individual resins, they have unique identities and structures, which change when they combine. As epoxy glue they not only stick to each other, but they hold other objects together as well. This shared purpose may be worth giving up some of their individuality. Like these resins, student affairs may need to sacrifice its unique identity to create a stronger union with others in the academy.

We are living in a networked world with connections growing by the minute. These connections are being fueled by the growing role of technology in our lives, the impact of mass media, and the global economy. Shifts on a global scale are also reshaping the way organizations operate. Computer networks, e-mail, and informal relationships are creating a human and technological web that overlays the traditional hierarchy. The hierarchy has not disappeared, but the way we work increasingly reflects a blurring of traditional divisional boundaries. People in a networked organization need to modify the way they relate to each other. This chapter will describe the importance of optimizing relationships and connections that reflect the underlying nature of organizations, the need to develop the kind of relational thinking that is different than the sequential causal chains of reasoning used in the past, and to see how emotions will play an increasing role in our work lives. These new ways of relating will require us to color outside the lines of our departments, blur the boundaries of our jobs, and like the two resins, combine with others to achieve a greater shared purpose.

A networked world operates on linkages, connections, and interdependencies. If this is a surprise, reflect on some of the connections we take so much for granted that they appear invisible. One January morning, Ron was traveling from Minneapolis to Tucson. When he arrived at the airport, he noticed there were more people than usual gathered in the terminal. As he stood in line to check in, he heard rumors of flights being canceled and noticed agents busily rerouting various travelers. People ahead of him were yelling at the agent, and a general level of anxiety was spreading like a virus through the airport. When he got to the counter, he asked the airline representative what was happening. "Snow storms in Philadelphia and New York," she said. He looked out the window—it was a beautiful, clear, winter day in Minnesota and, having checked the forecast, he knew the weather in Tucson was gorgeous. Snow in the east delayed or grounded planes needed in Minneapolis. Because Ron is a frequent traveler, this information was not too much of a surprise. He had learned from experience that many variables—both visible and invisible—could affect his travel plans. This story exemplifies how difficulties "at a distance" can affect a highly connected system.

This story is not an unusual one. Most of us who travel have experienced something similar at some point in time. However, it is an example of how we take for granted the many highly connected systems in our lives. If we began to list them, we would begin to wonder how we get anywhere on a fairly regular basis. For example, in the above story, some of the systems on which Ron depended included computer networks for ticketing and re-routing, weather systems, spaces available in airport parking lots, his car's mechanical system, traffic systems, his own biological systems, and the technical infrastructure systems like electricity and water, that support these other systems. Often it is only when something does not work that we reflect on the complex nature of these many interdependent systems. The focus on the Y2K computer bug at the end of the 20th Century raised our awareness of the many technical infrastructure systems we depend on and how a glitch in these systems can impact our lives.

On campuses, fall move-in days require that all the systems, both on- and off-campus, needed for individual students be in place. In this example, we recognize the various family systems needed to coordinate the packing and transportation of a son or daughter. Once on campus, the service systems of food, housing, orientation, registration, and billing, as well as the psychological and biological systems of each and every human being present, are involved. As parents and students interact with staff, the emotions of parting with their child coupled with the general frustrations of parking and unpacking contribute to the ease or challenges of move-in day. When seen in this complexity, it is a wonder it happens at all.

These examples demonstrate the interdependence that underlies many systems today. Systems theory describes how organizations consist of multiple networks with interdependent relationships. This understanding assumes that all components of an organization are naturally associated with each other. Individual components influence and are influenced by the actions of other components in the living system. Interdependence exists in a system if the movement of one part affects all the other parts of the system (Eoyang, 1993). Working in and understanding the interdependent nature of systems requires a relational perspective and function in order to be effective.

As student affairs practitioners, we have always had a relational aspect to our work. We relate to students, each other, outside constituents, and other colleagues. However, we have always been stronger at relating with students and each other than colleagues institution-wide. We need to become more conscious of the connections and interdependencies within universities. Most of us have been taught to understand connections through organizational structure. We see reporting lines, organizational charts, departments and divisions. However, in a connective system, the processes that ripple through the system often disregard the formal reporting lines, in the same way that a touch anywhere moves a whole spider web. In a networked knowledge era, it is helpful to view organizations as webs of relationships and processes in order to understand, shape, and effectively work within the system. To develop this elevated awareness and understanding of our institutions as webs of relationships, we need to become skilled at

• optimizing relationships and connections,
• relational thinking,
• understanding emotional dynamics, and
• practicing new ways of relating.

Optimizing Relationships and Connections

The reality for most institutions is fragmentation, wherein individuals are often unaware of the overall system. However, this perception of being a separate autonomous part is an illusion because, despite our ignorance of the rest of the organization, what we do in our various divisions still affects the whole system. In our capacity to effect institutional change, we need to go farther by nurturing a broader range of relationships and developing new interdependencies in organizational systems. Optimizing relationships involves seeking and incorporating diverse ideas and perspectives, developing meaningful cross-boundary relationships, and forming relationships based on trust and integrity. In a connected world, these skills take on a greater importance than ever before because one's value and effectiveness to an organization is directly proportional to one's relationship to the organization. Networked organizations work from the principle of connection, not separation.

Student affairs practitioners already tend to see things in terms of relationships when it comes to students. If we apply this lens to our organizations, we can see relationships and connections to others in the organization. There are potential allies in our organization for this kind of systemic viewing of our work. Business and institutional advancement colleagues also have a unique perspective that would enhance our ability to see institutions as a whole system. A new identity for student affairs staff is to think of themselves as conducting a symphony. This symphony, rather than creating music, is creating cross-boundary connections, sharing information widely, seeking diverse perspectives, developing relationships built on trust, and helping others to do the same. As the musical symphony is created by musicians playing their instruments harmoniously, the purpose of the student affairs "conductor" is to increase the institution's ability to create an interdependent community for the benefit of all, but especially students.

Becoming a facilitator of connections and information involves developing new partnerships. This requires increasing the amount of time we spend in relationship with others. Most of us believe that our "major" is the administration of our division and our "minor" is developing relationships within and beyond our division. If we want to create institutions that respond to the challenges of a networked environment, we need to switch our emphasis and put relationships at the core of our work. Margaret Wheatley (1995) delineates three ways to optimize relationships and connections in an organization: through facilitating relationships, making connections through the sharing of information, and continually reshaping our relationship to our organizational identity.

Relationships

Relationships are the connective tissue of the organization. Like the structures and muscles of our body, information, identity, and meaning are tied together through this medium. This connective tissue is important for a learning organization because relationships provide opportunities to create "networks and webs of dialogue in generative communication" (Marshall, 1996, p. 187). In networked organizations, relationships are sources of energy that sustain important efforts over time. The current infrastructure on most campuses does not nurture these relationships across divisional boundaries or in some cases even within divisions.

Using the ability to develop relationships with students, staff, and faculty should be a natural aspect of our daily student affairs practice. This ability can be used at multiple entry points on a college campus. For example, we can bring individuals who do not know each other into relationship, or we can facilitate new alliances and cooperative ventures with others. At another level, we can encourage departments or student groups to collaborate in new ways. Over time, these new relationships, built on trust and integrity, become the glue that holds us together. Each time we bring others together, create environments where people feel safe to share their perspectives, and listen to each other, we create a more holistic picture of the organization and the larger environment. In a networked world, this helps the organization become more adaptable over time.

The challenge in relationship building is that it is time-consuming. In addition, it is often difficult to cross institutional boundaries. Each of us has more than enough things to do without moving beyond our current departmental boundaries. However, fostering interdependencies requires us to prioritize relationships despite these difficulties. If we do not foster more relationships than we do currently, the institution will remain fragmented. This fragmentation is in part what is causing some of the difficulties in a "bounded" workspace. When a decision made at one end of the institution affects us, time is spent working through the negative effects of that decision on our department.

In addition to these tangible problems, the rumor mill often amplifies decisions within a fragmented and distrustful organization. Rumors increase in environments of distrust and people's responses to "decisions made at a distance" take on an emotional valence that hinders future cooperation and collaboration, resulting in the increase of fragmentation within an organization. However, if individuals who make decisions understand they are in relationship with others, they can discuss what they are thinking before they make decisions. The question is, where do we want to spend our time? Do we want to spend it minimizing the negative impact of a decision in which we were not involved, or fostering connections and relationships that decrease the time we spend in crisis management?

Information

If relationships are like the body's connective tissue, information is the circulatory system through which organizational life flows. In an organization, the circulatory system carries the life's blood and is necessary for continued health. Information is both "the underlying structure and dynamic process that insures life" (Wheatley, 1992, p. 102). It is the medium for generative organizational learning and center of organizational life. It brings energy and washes away impurities. Information is an organizational resource and is unique because of its ability to generate itself. We have all been surprised at how quickly information can travel in an organization, as well as its ability to transform into something entirely different from its initial meaning.

Most organizations do not see information as the lifeblood of the system. Instead of circulating it freely, we attempt to control, restrict, or manage data, knowledge, intelligence, and news. Wheatley (1996) views an organization as a living system which organically self-organizes with the help of information. In her understanding, restricting information also restricts the organization's ability to renew itself. The traditional paradigm of management believes that it is important to control the amount, timing, and direction of information. This belief complemented the hierarchical view in which management was differentiated from workers in part by the knowledge and information they held. Our continued attempts to control information may not only be damaging our organization's ability to learn, but may also be impossible to maintain. Helgesen (1995) states that

> *"... information technology destroys an organization's long-held notions of who has sufficient information to make important decisions, and who does not. It takes away the distinctions between heads and hands, between those who think and those who do, and makes it impossible for us not to notice, as Henry Mintzberg has observed, that 'people at the so-called bottom in organizations have heads too, in fact often very good ones'" (p. 14).*

Controlling information appears possible when organizations are viewed mechanistically; however, if we see organizations as a series of linked networks (like the Internet), information is uncontrollable and necessary for the health of the system. Therefore, information sharing instead of withholding becomes important to sustain a networked organization, just as an organ denied blood becomes necrotic. Information sharing facilitates cross-boundary relationships and understanding. Over time, freely circulating information also develops trust within an organization.

Student affairs professionals have some appreciation of information flow and its effect on students' development. We realize when students do not receive feedback on their behavior, it can hinder their development. Student conduct hearings, confronting a roommate with a problem, and agendas at student meetings are all designed to open up feedback loops. As a whole, student affairs practitioners need to become more aware of how information can be used to facilitate transformation on their campuses. We need to take what we apply in selected student development situations and extend it to an institutional level. We do not need to move information along a channel or see it as a step-by-step process that flows downward or upward in the organization. Rather, we need to share information and use it to generate new knowledge, to create open and multiple pathways for communication, and to promote dialogue, interactions, and feedback. The power of meaningful conversations to change an organization should not be underestimated.

Identity

Identity becomes the third dimension that gets shaped through the free exchange of information and relationships. If relationships are the connective tissue and information is the circulatory system, identity is the shape of the whole. For example, when an organization shares information about the challenges facing a college campus today and the members of that campus hold meaningful dialogues about these challenges, their understanding of themselves increases. This understanding becomes the basis for a shared identity that is evolving in relationship to their external environment and new information. In a networked world, our identity needs to be based in interdependent relationships, not in separated parts.

Institutions organize themselves around identity (Wheatley & Kellner-Rogers, 1996). For example, a community college president brought in a variety of emergent thinkers in order to generate dialogue on the future of his institution. These thinkers met with trustees, faculty, and staff to share ideas for a number of years. The dialogues triggered new thinking about the college and its vision of itself. The college's identity is shifting as a result of the information that is being shared. This, in turn, brings the college into relationship with the external environment in new and different ways.

The Interactive Effect

Relationships, information, and identity have an interactive effect on each other. One example of optimizing relationships and connections occurred in a large, very diverse, research university through their redefinition process of the student service areas. They reviewed enrollment, financial aid, and admissions services throughout the university. They brought staff together from many areas of the institution and created many new relationships. One of the oft-heard quotes was "I've seen the name, but never the person." Relationships among staff were further expanded and information was generated and shared through meetings, development of process maps, and other ways. This process shaped the identity of what these services will look like in the future, created a new vision and standard of student services, and even reduced costs! The question is, did the identity change as a result of the new relationships and information, or was the vision of bringing people and information together in new ways actually the beginning of a new identity? The answer to this question is moot. All three aspects of relationships, information, and vision were used to trigger change. As a result, they mutually shaped and affected each other. This constant forming and reforming process continues to shape new relationships, information, and identity in a mutual interaction.

Relationships help us to understand who we are in a different way. New information brings us into relationship with others and in turn shapes our identity. Then, as we begin to think about who we are in different ways, we develop relationships that match that identity and we seek out information that supports this new identity. If student affairs practitioners chose to see their purpose as fostering relationships and sharing information, they would shape their day's work differently. This new approach, in turn, would affect our identity within the institution and the field. The interactions among all three suggest that we can develop stronger, connective understanding of organizations if we bring people into relationship with each other, share information widely, and have ongoing conversations about who we are.

Relational Thinking

New ways of relating go beyond building human networks to a new way of thinking. In highly connected systems, the distinction between independent and dependent variables becomes blurred and can only be understood if we think rationally. We are used to linear causal chains of logic which fit nicely into hierarchical organizations. However, networks do not work that way. In networks there are many variables in play and the impact of these variables cannot always be immediately seen for several reasons.

First, there are too many variables in play. As mentioned in Chapter One, the weather is a perfect example of this principle. Many variables go into developing a model that predicts the weather. However, at best the prediction is rarely exact, in part due to the multiplicity of variables that affect the weather. This is not a problem for us, because we understand that weather predictions tell us what is likely, not what is guaranteed. The same is true in networked systems. As connections increase, the numbers of variables in play also increases.

This explains why single causality does not work in networks: connections trigger dynamic movement. The more connections a system has, the more variables there are that can affect the system over time. As variables and connections increase, there is more movement within the system, which in turn leads to greater complexity. The Internet is a good example of this. As more and more people come on line, the number of portals, web sites, information, diversity of services, and active players on the Internet increases. Each of these variables changes everyday, creating a constant dynamic quality to the Internet. This movement makes the Internet difficult to accurately describe on any one day. The dynamic nature of the Internet is due in part to the increasing complexity of the relationships between and among variables on the Internet.

Third, more variables and greater dynamic movement in a network create impact from a distance. When many variables, connected within a system create dynamic movement, the impact on a specific location may not be traceable back to its original point of effect. Retention is a perfect example of this. There are many variables that contribute to students' decisions to stay or persist in college. When a college has a good retention year, the temptation is to give credit to one or two strategies, but most practitioners know that giving credit to one strategy does not accurately represent the complexity of the variables that affect college retention. The reality is that institutional strategies, national financial aid policies, the global economy, or all of the above in various combinations could have impacted good retention.

Networks do not reward traditional logic because there are too many variables in play, which trigger dynamic movement and make it difficult to track cause and effect over time. This reality of networks has one major implication in how we think. We need to shift from a sequential cause and effect model of understanding the world to a relational thinking process. In order to understand a complex dynamic system, we need to search for the key variables and work to understand their relationship to each other as well as what the likely second and third order implications are over time. Dörner (1996), in his book *The Logic of Failure*, states that one of the primary reasons that strategic planning fails is that planners succumb to the temptation of using one or two independent variables to focus on, disregarding the relationships among the multiple variables in play in their environment. We need to increase the complexity of our thinking process. Look for the relationships between and among these variables over time. If we can change our thinking habits, we can more effectively understand the relational nature of a networked world. Relational thinking is being used in retention models, influencing residence hall cultures, and in substance abuse interventions. In these situations, we have given up belief in the "one best" intervention strategy and spent time understanding the many variables in play and their relationships to each other. We use this knowledge to develop a holistic approach to the system we want to influence. This understanding of the relational nature of a networked world also involves a greater understanding of why emotions have become more prevalent in our organizations.

Understanding Emotional Dynamics

Traditionally, emotions have not had a place in organizations. Work was a place of rationality. However, this has begun to change. Now words with emotional implications, such as commitment, excitement, passion, and celebration have found their way into organizational language. However the acceptance of these positive emotions has not led to an ability to address negative ones within an organization. We talk about cynicism, fear, withdrawal, and negative attitudes as forces to be wiped out in organizations and the people who demonstrate these behaviors are seen as a liability.

This approach-avoidance response to emotions is about to be challenged due to the nature of networked systems. Networks facilitate the spread of emotions within an organization because networks do not restrict their connections to rational information—they spread everything, including the emotions of the people sharing information. Research in communication states that tonality and other non-verbal behavior has a greater impact on communication than words. This phenomenon is amplified within a networked system—technological or human. Therefore more emotions will shape communications within organizations. The mass media are good examples of this phenomenon. While journalism standards suggest that the news should be an unbiased reporting of the facts, the reality is that most of the nightly news and television news magazines have blurred the lines between factual reporting and entertainment, which is filled with emotions.

Sometimes communication that is given in a factual form can be interpreted emotionally in a networked system. An example of this is an e-mail message. Electronic mail has the illusion of communicating information without emotions. However, it does not actually work that way. The emotional state of the sender (frustrated, frazzled, fed-up) shapes the phases, word choices, and length of the message. The emotional state of the receiver (defensive, sensitive, stressed) becomes a lens through which the message is interpreted. This can lead to misunderstandings and result in the forwarding of the e-mail exchange to various colleagues. These exchanges combine to amplify the emotional responses rather than the rational.

The nature of emotional communication and the speed at which it spreads within a system are not a new concept to student affairs practitioners. As resident directors, student activities advisors, or directors of ethnic centers, we have plenty of experience on how emotions spread within a residence hall, a programming board, or an ethnic student organization. It is a natural occurrence with our students. We see our job, in part, as helping students learn to manage their emotions and sort out the facts from the emotions of the situation. However, we usually are not prepared to experience this phenomenon with faculty and staff within our institutions.

In a networked organization, emotions are a natural part of the system and can consume a great deal of time. For example, if there is little trust within a division or institution, everything becomes emotional. This leads to rumors and increased crises. This reality has a major implication for us—we simply need to become more sophisticated at managing our emotions. Daniel Goleman (1998) in his book *Working with Emotional Intelligence* states that having a more emotionally intelligent work place can dramatically increase our ability to productively collaborate with each other. According to Goleman "emotional intelligence refers to the capacity for recognizing our own feelings and those of others, for motivating ourselves, and for managing emotions well in ourselves and in our relationships" (p. 317). When individuals are emotionally intelligent, they have self-knowledge, can manage their own emotions, have empathy, and are sensitive to group dynamics. In a networked organization where emotionality is flowing freely, we may need to require greater degrees of emotional intelligence in all employees.

Practicing New Ways of Relating

If we bring to our student affairs work a commitment to a new role in which we influence the organization to think about and practice new ways of relating, we can make a significant difference—wherever we may be in our organizations—by modeling and fostering the following:

1. *Fostering a trusting environment where people can speak honestly about what they see and experience.* In order to understand the system, we need to receive information from the people in the organization. If they are restricting information upward in the organization, the positional leaders will never have a true picture of what is happening. We need to foster an environment where people believe they can speak honestly about what they see and experience. Modeling trust and integrity is critical to fostering a trusting environment.

2. *Developing one's own emotional intelligence and helping develop it in others.* Develop a greater awareness of yourself and your reactions to situations. Learn to manage your emotions, develop the ability to empathize with others, and master group and social dynamics. These capacities will be important to maintaining your own centeredness. As we develop these capacities in ourselves, we need to facilitate the development of emotional intelligence in others.

3. *Sharing information widely.* Communicate and share information about what we are doing and elicit information from others. For example, having regular staff meetings within student affairs is a natural forum for the distribution, sharing, and discussion of institutional information. Creating all-campus forums to discuss important issues is another way to spread information widely. Involving other departments in dialogues on key topics can also generate more shared information in the system. Many of us need information that academic and administrative offices have about issues that affect students. In turn, student affairs staff have information that is relevant to colleagues in academic and administrative services. Sharing relevant

information with each other extends the number of people who have a larger understanding of the systemic issues affecting the students' learning process. This sharing creates a natural dynamic that brings the system into relationship and begins to foster questions about our identity as institutions of higher education. However, this practice has a paradox embedded in it. While we need to share information widely, we also need to be careful about what information we pass on. Since the system is connective, information can move "untouched" through the organization; as such, misinformation can be generated as easily as relevant information. For instance, when we pass on a rumor without checking the facts, we can unintentionally add to the confusion about what is accurate.

4. *Engaging in boundary spanning activities.* We need to engage in cross-boundary discussions as a regular part of our practice. Our institutions are made up of complex connective systems. If we do not engage in ongoing dialogues about the impact of our decisions on the whole system, we will likely experience unintended consequences, as well as the intended ones. These unintended consequences may be negative, neutral, or positive. Cross-boundary discussions help us to see the whole and more accurately understand all the ramifications of a decision.

As comfortable as boundaries are, they also are prisons. When we protect the territory, marking it out, telling everybody else to stay away, we inhibit our organization's ability to thrive in a connective world. Our body is held together with interstitial tissue. This tissue connects our skeleton with muscles and is necessary for coordinated movement. The interstitial space of an organization is found at the boundaries of our territories. It is where various parts of the organization connect with each other through relationships and sharing information. Solid, protected boundaries actually hinder us from helping the organization see itself as a whole system. This perspective challenges us to be more open and share information more widely.

5. *Intentionally creating new relationships.* What would happen if you spent time creating a new relationship every week? A career development director made it her goal to attend each department's faculty meeting over a three-year period. This strategy created a vast number of new relationships that have begun to shape how faculty at her college view connections between their work and career preparation for their students. Leadership in an organization that recognizes and depends on the health of its relationships needs to function in part like a janitor. A janitor clears hallways in the same way that a leader

clears networks and channels between people and ideas. We need to develop infrastructures that facilitate interaction between people and departments.

6. *Creating relational instead of organizational charts.* Most of us chart an organization by its structure. When we orient students or describe the structure to new staff members, we use a functional chart filled with boxes and lines. Organizations are comprised of interdependent relationships, and therefore, need to be understood as relational entities. People accomplish organizational functions. Many employees know more and do more than their specific job description. Our success is dependent in part on finding and building relationships with these rich sources of information and ability. This information is usually learned by happenstance and chance. Some supervisors have learned through trial and error that òne effective way of training new staff is by giving them a list of people to meet. This strategy intuitively recognizes that our work gets done through people. What would we see if we drew an organizational relationship map?

7. *Looking for "families" of solutions for interdependent problems.* We have understood this concept intuitively for many years. Initially we searched for the one perfect solution that would solve alcohol abuse on our campuses. Now we realize that alcohol use and abuse is a highly complex, interdependent phenomenon, needing a combination of solutions that are simultaneously implemented. We need to extend this kind of awareness to other problems that are interconnected. Retention, leadership development, and fostering a multi-cultural environment are all additional examples of a "family" of complex, dynamic, interdependent issues.

8. *Learning to accept the complexities of the system.* Organizations are living systems and as such, operate with many more layers of complexity than we can truly understand. In these systems, amazing events and natural accidents are normal. For example, when things go wrong, it may be due to system complexity instead of individual error. These kinds of complex connective systems are fragile even though they work most of the time. Any of us who have a networked computer system on our campus has experienced these kinds of natural accidents. Familiar phrases like, "The system is slow today," "The system is down and we do not know exactly what's causing it," "That problem is not supposed to happen," are all examples of the novel problems that arise from complex systems. These problems are not the fault of any one individual, but a result of the emergent properties that arise from a complex highly-connected system. As is also

the case when "organizational accidents" occur, it is not helpful to blame individuals in the organization. The best strategy is to accept the accident and spend energy on finding the solution.

9. *Infusing the organization with abundant feedback.* Feedback is needed to create a "pinch" in an individual or an organization, which in turn creates pressure to change. When all levels of institutions receive relevant information, they build a greater ability to adapt to the larger system. As individuals and departments receive feedback, they initiate appropriate and positive change without waiting for the vice president to tell them what to do. When individuals take initiative to respond to change, the flexibility of the organization increases. Sharing information widely is antithetical to traditional management strategy that generally restricts information to people in positions. Providing information across the board allows employees to openly engage with the larger system and actively respond to it, thereby generating and continuing feedback loops back to the larger system, which shape the next round of possibilities. This dynamic exchange continues to spiral into the future creating multiple opportunities to mutually shape the environment and the organization.

In a connected system, practitioners cannot go back to autonomous work. Both the ability and the responsibility to use our relating skills institution-wide is needed because it is one of the key ways we can strengthen the learning environment for students. If we can model interdependent relationships on our current campuses, then students will think and act interdependently instead of autonomously. This modeling can help them be more successful in the future and provide them with the skills to make a bigger difference in the world.

At the beginning of this chapter, we described how two resins became epoxy glue when they united their molecules, thus changing their individual identities. They became the glue that held other parts together. Student affairs could have a similar kind of future if its practitioners thought of themselves as institutional glue. If the student affairs profession shifts its work to include *optimizing relationships and connections, facilitating relational thinking, understanding emotional dynamics, and practicing new ways of relating*, it can help institutions to respond to the needs and challenges of a networked world. This shift in turn, will help students respond successfully to the challenges of the external environment. While this will not be a simple, quick, or easy process, it is a special and noble task worthy of our strongest efforts.

Reflective Questions:

1. What information do I have that may be of value to others at my college?
2. What barriers are currently in place restricting the flow of information?
3. What are our formal relationships and do they honestly reflect how we get the work done?
4. What are the real relationships through which we are often most effective?
5. Do we have a shared understanding of who we are as a division of student affairs, and as a college or university?
6. Are we working from the same sense of shared purpose? How do we know?
7. What would a college that shares information widely look like?
8. What systems would help support the forming of new relationships and sharing of information?
9. What could happen if student affairs continues to defend and protect its boundaries in a boundariless organization?
10. If your value in a connective world is related to your interdependence, what value does an autonomous division have to the whole college?
11. How do we train professionals to understand and practice student affairs from an interdependent perspective?
12. If you are working with people who do not recognize interdependence, how do you help change their worldviews?
13. How do we help change the way our organization operates to include interdependence?
14. How does leadership change in an interdependent system?
15. How does the concept of the leader/follower relationship change under conditions of interdependency?

Chapter 3

New Ways of Influencing Change

"Everything is in a constant process of discovery and creating. Everything is changing all the time: Individuals, systems, environments, the rules, and the processes of evolution. Even change changes."
— Wheatley & Kellner-Rogers

The manner in which change is "influenced" within a networked organization is different from the manner in which change is "created" within a traditional, non-networked organization. Networked systems work with different rules and require different strategies to make effective change. But one thing that has not changed is how individuals think about change in our organizations. Current rules for making change in organizations have evolved from the nature of hierarchies. However, if our organizations are beginning to function more like an ecological web than a pyramid, the change strategies we are most familiar with may actually be less effective.

Living in a connected world shifts both the dynamics of how things change and the way we can trigger change in the organization. Our challenge is to become better at triggering change to help bring about the kind of deep transformation needed in higher education. In this chapter, we will describe

• the shifting dynamics of change,
• different approaches we need to use to influence change, and
• how to optimize our influence in an interconnected world.

The Shifting Dynamics of Change: From Hierarchies to Networks

Shifts occurring in society are changing the way things change. Instantaneous communication fed by technology has the effect of shrinking time. Technology is also fueling greater connectivity and is putting everything and everyone in relationship with one another. The accessibility to and availability of information is also magnified through mass media and technology. Everything is connected to everything else. This can, at times, be overwhelming particularly when connectivity increases a sense of urgency or accelerates the need for an immediate response.

The sense of diminishing time to respond to change or the need for an immediate response can cause frustration. Much of this frustration is founded in either the organization's inflexibility, an individual's inability to be open to change or both. We have all been taught the traditional dynamics of change. However, technology continues to fuel a trend in which the world is becoming more connected and information and knowledge are becoming more important for organizational renewal and learning. Seeking out new ways to influence change in organizations is important in order to help institutions respond to today's pressing issues. The following section describes how the strategies that networks and hierarchies use to create change operate simultaneously in organizations.

The Nature of Change in Hierarchies

Every day at work we are confronted with multiple assumptions of how change occurs in our organizations and how we can influence this change. Students demand immediate results and if they do not occur, they take their problems to the next level. The current strategy of creating "one-stop service" on college campuses is one response to this growing demand for immediate service on the part of students. Students assume that change can happen immediately. On the other hand, business, academic, and student affairs administrators believe that change takes time and needs to be planned out in detail. White papers, ad hoc committees and strategic planning processes—designed to study the problem, make recommendations, and implement change—are current practices of how we attempt to create change on campuses.

Assumptions about the dynamics of the change process affect how we attempt to shape change in organizations. Most of us have lived our lives working in hierarchical organizations. It is through this experience that we have learned the rules governing organizational change. The nature of a hierarchy is embedded in the image of a pyramid. There are a lot of people at the bottom of the organization and these people report to others, who in turn report to others. In each layer of reporting structure there are fewer supervisors until we get to the top of the organization where there is one president. This individual is empowered to set the vision and direct the actions of the total organization. The natural order of a hierarchy is built on parts; each part links with another part, which in turn links serially with the rest of the organization. The person at the top understands and directs the interrelationship of these many parts. The image evoked is an individual standing on top of a pyramid with a bird's eye view of both the organization and the surrounding territory. The assumption is that they see things the rest of us can not, which might explain why we listen so attentively to presidents.

Hierarchies, built on serial linkages, also support the assumption that linchpins in the form of positional managers know more than the people below them. Over time, this assumption is supported by a variety of infrastructures like performance appraisal systems, decision-making structures, and recognition systems, which reinforce a dependency relationship between workers and their supervisor. Hierarchies are designed to run on positional power, with the person at the top having more power than the people right below him or her and so on down through the system. This is one reason people in hierarchies assume that change cannot occur unless the person at the top initiates it. This perception is reinforced by the dependency relationship people have with positional managers. The nature of a hierarchy is to reinforce this dependency because it is easier for one person to get things done if others in the organization will do what he/she asks. While most of us can relate to the nature of hierarchies, we also know there are limits to their effectiveness in creating meaningful change.

The Nature of Change in Networks

The nature of networks operates very differently from a hierarchy. Think again about how the Internet might look if one were to draw it. There is a series of nodes, each with its own network, connected to multiple nodes. Communication among nodes and between nodes and their networks is rapid and fluid, often taking many routes to a destination. One person cannot control the network by nature because there are many active players with their own networks. In fact, it would be impossible to control the Internet. For example, if an individual successfully eliminated information coming from one web-site, another web-site could easily provide this information. The nature of a network is always changing, shifting, and in dynamic flux. A network cannot be forced to follow a specific set course because the interconnections allow for many different ways to get from one place to another. On the Internet, the bits of information in an e-mail message are sent through many different routes and reassembled at their destination.

Information, energy, and activities flow through a system in constantly changing configurations. In this sense the system is fluid and works like a living organism. We can see this dynamic in nature. When a stream is blocked by a rock, at first the water backs up behind it; when enough pressure is built up, the stream finds an alternate route around the rock. In a web, if one's original connection is removed, the network finds and creates alternative routes to reach its destination.

Change strategies of coercion or force do not work in a network. If forced, the network resists the attempt at control. If we want to influence a network, we need to understand the dynamics of a network. Networks are open to influence when multiple individuals intentionally nudge the system from multiple directions. These influencing strategies have to have a rhythm of nudging and waiting, nudging and waiting. A network takes time to respond. When individuals come together to nudge the system to accomplish a specific goal, they need to build in a time-delay to give the system time to respond. Then they nudge again.

A networked world is filled with sets of interconnecting web-like systems. When any sub-system nudges the larger system, it creates a ripple effect on the whole system. At any one time, there are always multiple changes that are being made in the system. This increases the complexity of understanding the whole system. Any sub-group can initiate change in the system, and the ripple effects of their change strategies can affect the system at a substantial distance from the initial point of impact. Web-like systems make cause and effect difficult to track. This is a very different dynamic than the person at the top of the organization triggering all change.

Dynamic Tensions between Hierarchies and Networks

The dynamics of change in hierarchies involve top-down initiation, the use of positional power to ensure action, and the fostering of dependency relationships. A hierarchy assumes that the source of intelligence is at the top of the organization and the people at the bottom of the organization are the receivers of information. This is like the traditional broadcast system in television. The source of intelligence and decision making power resides with the executives in the TV studios and their programming decisions are broadcast downward through the system. The dynamics of change in a network involve influencing from multiple points using gentle nudges with time-outs for the system to respond and mutually shape the direction. There is an overabundance of information spread widely throughout a system like the Internet.

Therefore, the source of intelligence shifts to the individuals at the receiving end of the Internet. Each person decides what information to draw down from the wide variety of choices available (Negroponte, 1995). In a networked system, intelligence exists everywhere in the system, not just at the top of the organization. This shifts the dynamics of change. If intelligence exists at all points within a system, then choices, decisions, and initiation can occur from anywhere in the system. They organize themselves around shared values, vision, and purpose. No one is waiting to be told what to think or do.

These two very different dynamics of change are embedded in the nature of hierarchies and networks and are summarized in Table 3.1. Most of us live with the tension between these two approaches to change. Many of us work in hierarchical organizations and also experience a second reality in which the organization functions increasingly like a network, a duality that leads to conflicting ideas about change strategies. This reality may seem far off for some, but for those of us working in institutions with computer networks, which connect students, staff and faculty, it is already here. Our challenge today is to live with the tensions that these two systems create; our challenge tomorrow is to use these insights to trigger change more effectively so we can engage organizations in the deep transformational change needed in higher education.

How Change is Effected in Hierarchies and Networks

Dynamics of change in hierarchies	Dynamics of change in networks
Change is initiated at the top	Change is initiated from anywhere
The source of intelligence comes from head of the organization	The source of intelligence exists throughout the organization
Change occurs through forceful sustained progress toward a specific goal	Change occurs through a coordinated nudging and waiting by many people intentionally influencing toward a shared goal

Table 3.1

Our very beliefs about how we influence change must change. We live in a highly complex system. Even the way things change is changing. Change is no longer incremental; it can now occur by either small steps or giant leaps. In fact, student affairs practitioners have a lot of experience with this reality of change. Despite how our world is increasingly filled with interconnections and discontinuous leaps, student affairs educators have found ways of influencing and impacting students' lives just the same. The added opportunity exists to develop a greater awareness of what we have learned about the dynamics of change from our experiences. We can also develop a greater understanding of different approaches to change. Once this awareness is gained, we can help the entire institution to understand and influence change in our work world.

Different Approaches to Change

One of the emergent capacities needed for systemic leadership is paradigm cognition, which is defined as being able to recognize when different paradigms are most useful and shift behavior accordingly. It will be increasingly important for us to become skilled at recognizing the underlying belief systems (our paradigms) we have about change and intentionally match our change strategies to the context in which we are working. We believe there are three different ways that we use to influence the dynamics of change on an organizational and individual level. These three approaches are *making change, surviving change, and organic change*. Each of these approaches has different focuses and values and each creates meaning in different ways.

The hierarchical approach of *making change reflects the assumption that change is predictable and controllable*. The approach of *surviving change has been triggered by the increase of interruptions, novel problems, and crises in our day-to-day lives*. As these events occur more regularly in our workday, student affairs practitioners have become more skilled in adapting to the kind of unpredictability that often reflects our work. Becoming skilled at surviving, however, does not allow us to impact change as we believed we could in the past. It also creates a certain level of frustration at a time when influencing our future is critical. If we continue to work in a survival mode under conditions of turbulent change, we will eventually be consumed by mounting stress and burn out. It is much like rowing up stream against a strong current. It is very tiring work with not much progress to show for it. As society becomes increasingly more complex, surviving is not enough and yet paradoxically it seems to be the only answer. *The organic change approach challenges us to evolve beyond surviving rapid change to learning how to trigger organic change within a networked environment*. We have a choice to make. Do we want to actively shape our future, or do we want to just survive our future?

The different approaches to change as summarized in Table 3.2 are designed to help us understand the assumptions we have held about change and juxtapose the focuses used in the past and use in the present with those needed for the future. The table compares the focus of change, organizational values, and meaning making.

Different Approaches to Change

Making Change	Surviving Change	Organic Change
Focus of change: Forcing or driving change through the system by positional power. The organization is insular and change comes from within. Example: "Change has to come from the top"	*Focus of change:* Surviving change that is forced upon us from external forces. Example: Scanning environment is added to strategically protect and respond to outside threats.	*Focus of change:* Influencing the system through organic strategies. Increase organization's ability to respond quickly to change. Become a learning organization. Example: Intentional multi-directional influencing.
Organization values: Predictable and controlled change; individuals who are enthusiastic about the organization's goals. Example: Long range plans; "buy in" to organizational goals.	*Organization values:* Increasing organizational capacity to survive. Constantly adjusting to environmental conditions; developing individual ways of coping with change. Example: "Do more with less"; crisis management training.	*Organization values:* New ways of relating, new ways of influencing change, and new ways of learning. Example: "Do business differently"; develop strategic partnerships.
Meaning making: Found in predictable patterns and staying on purpose; clear picture of result; belief that if we accomplish this change we will succeed. Example: Mission statements.	*Meaning making:* Found in threats and opportunities that emerge as patterns in larger environment; belief that we can survive this. Example: Studying national trends on student demographics.	*Meaning making:* Found in relational thinking; belief that collective intelligence and innovations will lead us to new ways of influencing the system. Example: Integrated learning; perpetual innovation.

Table 3.2

Making Change

Making change requires the use of force or positional power to push change though the system and control the change process. Organizations that "make change" are filled with individuals and infrastructures, which help to control their people or destiny. On good days, these principles help maintain the stability of the organization. On bad days, being overly controlled can reduce or eliminate creativity. An organization that "makes change" initiates it from the top moving downward, often in an incremental fashion. It is important when working from this approach to maintain control over the pace and process of change. These principles are familiar to us because we have experience with them. Most of us have been trained in these techniques and even advocated the need to have order and control in the organization.

Focus of Change: In order to control the dynamics of change, one has to be able to remain autonomous from outside influences. If an organization cannot remain autonomous from its outside environment, controlling the need and direction of change becomes a primary internal focus. Therefore, strategies to keep the organization as self-sufficient as possible are an important focus of change. Managing change involves developing strategies to remain in control or repairing the broken parts so that the organization can come back on-line as soon as possible (Bolman & Deal, 1984). Change strategies are often embedded in long-term planning or setting goals and objectives. These kinds of strategies maintain the illusion that change is a rational, linear, controlled event. For some organizations, this focus of change helps the members feel a sense of security because change becomes routinized.

When change is needed, the solution usually requires the organization to add resources to manage the new program. This strategy has its roots in the mechanistic assumptions that form the basis of a control and stability approach to change. A machine has difficulty radically altering its basic function. However, there are option packages or various parts that can be enhanced in a machine. An organization whose focus on change comes from control might solve an organizational problem by identifying a specific enhancement that would fix a part of the organization that has broken down. The specific enhancement usually costs money. For instance, if traffic continues to increase, the freeways become more and more congested. In the making change approach, the solution to the congestion is to add additional lanes, encourage car-pooling, or build a new freeway.

Organizational Values: When an organization uses the making change approach, it values its ability to control the change process. This leads to an appreciation of individuals who have an enthusiasm for the organization's goals. When people are committed to the value of stability, they work to see how they fit into the larger organization. Managers who are making change believe that their success as managers is related to their ability to reinforce order, resist disorder, and in some instances create an illusion of control.

These values usually exist to some degree in all organizations. In higher education, a common phrase, "don't rock the boat," alludes to the value placed on stability in the organization. When an organization values control, experimentation can be risky for the people or departments who make mistakes. Phrases such as "it's better to be safe than sorry" or "don't stick your neck out, it might get cut off" are other reflections of what the organizational culture rewards. New ideas or programs take time to implement because minimizing the risk involves getting approval all the way up the line. This long, drawn-out process weeds out proposals that have not been thought out at length and controls the rate of change at the same time.

Meaning Making: In organizations who use a making change approach, meaning is found in patterns that lead them to believe that change can be predicted and a controllable strategy can be designed to achieve the change they desire. Staff members who work for these kinds of organizations would find meaning in the belief that if they accomplish this change, the organization will be successful. Often this success is defined as beating the competition and strengthening the company. Rules of change provide a sense of stability and are defended because of their form, not just their substance. These rules might include beliefs that "change starts at the top" or "management knows best." Student affairs practitioners operating from this approach create change through policy development. This change strategy suggests that for every new problem one should write procedures, policies, or handbooks that spell out standardized responses. It is easy to see how bureaucracy can grow when one is making change with this level of control and predictability in mind.

Why this Approach is Not Enough: One of the benefits of forcing change down from the top includes a feeling of confidence and competence that comes from "being in charge" of one's own destiny. However, there are severe limitations to using this approach in today's environment. First, the making change approach takes time to think through and plan, which hinders one's ability to respond quickly to changing

environments. Second, this change approach assumes that an organization can control its environment, which is no longer a valid assumption
for most organizations. Third, a complex networked world needs perspectives from many individuals in order to be understood. The making
change approach depends on the head of the organization to initiate
change and see the need for change, but in a networked world no one
individual can fully understand a complex environment.

Surviving Change

Today, most student affairs organizations are challenged to re-think the
practices that flow from control and stability. However, their strategies
are often constrained by preexisting organizational assumptions that are
not working. The pace of our world no longer fits the organizational
principles of control and stability. This leads to frustrations as we hun-
ker down against the ill winds of change. Eventually, we adopt a survival mentality that better fits our changing context. New organizing
principles have evolved that center on surviving a turbulent environment. Control and stability are no longer possible and in response, many
of us focus on surviving the daily turbulence we experience.

Focus of Change: We have drawn from our experiences with weather
to help us understand how organizations can survive. Weather systems
are constantly changing. Some areas have greater variation, others have
more natural disasters, and others experience instantaneous shifts in the
weather. For instance, there is an old saying in St. Louis: "If you don't
like the weather now, wait 15 minutes." In adapting to the weather, we
take a survival approach. In Minnesota, people talk about how they
coped and survived the coldest winter on record or the time they made
it through the Halloween blizzard of 1991. They adapted by adding layers of clothes and learning to ski in the winter. All are ways to adapt and
acquiesce to the changing seasons. Organizations that design for survival have qualities of both machine and weather metaphors. While
hoping for some control, practitioners are savvy enough to realize that
change is going to show up in their work, usually from outside the
organization. Therefore, long-range planning has evolved into strategic
planning to accommodate changes in the environment.

Student affairs practitioners also take more time to scan the environment in an effort to have some advance warning of change. This
advance warning allows us to circle the wagons or mount a defense to
minimize the impact of change. An example of this is the national lob-
bying effort, launched in the spring of 1995 to minimize changes in fed-
eral financial aid. Organizational restructuring, downsizing, and right-

sizing have become common ways divisions move away from bureau-cratic structures in an effort to continually improve quality and to respond to budget cuts (Hammer & Champy, 1993).

Organizational Values: It is difficult to keep moving against the turbu-lent waters of change; however, many organizations are attempting to do just that. An organization that uses "surviving change" as its approach values anything or anyone that increases its capacity to respond to pressures from the external environment. In recent years, cri-sis-response teams, student-response teams, organizational restructur-ing, strategic analysis, and other strategies designed to increase both the quality of response and flexibility have found their way into our work environments. Staff get trained in crisis management and talking to the media. Individuals who are flexible and can adjust to change are also valued in contrast to staff that resist change or are not able to retrain themselves to meet the next challenge. This is also true for departments. The phrase "do more with less" is symptomatic of these organizational values.

Meaning Making: Newsletters, electronic bulletin boards, and confer-ence speakers help identify national trends and make meaning of an endless stream of data and events. These sources of information are vehicles for organizations to make sense of their environment. Managers seek meaning in patterns and national trends that might help them understand their local environment. In this environment, pattern recognition becomes an essential tool for understanding growing prob-lems and national trends before they show up on our desks.

Why this Approach is Not Enough: Higher education has too important a role in society to have its work shaped only by external forces. The debate about students being clients or products embodies the tension between customer service pressures and higher education's traditional role of character building and imparting wisdom for a lifetime. If we seek to satisfy the needs of students, we may not challenge them enough to become contributors to the future. Our work with students requires that we actively influence their learning, not just teach what they want. Similarly, organizations miss something if they just respond to external pressures and do not actively shape the community as well.

In addition to the costs to students and the future society, adherence to this approach results in a direct cost to the organization and its employ-ees. A survival mentality brings with it an egocentric view; institutions look out the window of the academy to see what is happening around them and focus on ways to cope with change while being unaware of the personal costs of stress, losing positions, conflicts between person-al and work expectations, and the loss of deeper meaning and purpose. There can be a sense of satisfaction and accomplishment in responding to day-to-day crises; in fact, sometimes it feels like the most tangible work we do. However, reacting is not enough. Continuing to work in a survival mode causes frustration and stress, which can result in profes-sional or personal burnout. It is frustrating when we spend our time reacting to change rather than creating the needed change. Absence of progress can result in the loss of hope.

Organic Change

Even if we cannot actually control the change process or the timing of change in our lives, we still want to know we can have a positive impact on the environment. Organic change uses a networked system to active-ly shape the outcomes we seek. Active influencing is an attempt to opti-mize the best of both approaches and embrace the differences as com-plementary opposites. For example, the tensions between controlling and surviving will never go away, but holding them in balance allows us to see a third way of working. This third way recognizes that while we cannot control the system, we are connected to it. Since we are part of the system, we can influence it if we learn how.

Focus of Change: Organic change requires a systemic focus. In a net-worked world, change occurs differently. Influencing is valued above controlling and the more influencing strategies used to nudge the sys-tem in a common direction, the better. This is a shift from the linear step-by-step focus of linear change strategies. Change is considered a mental as well as a physical activity. When people change their ideas of organizations, have more information, and learn together, they are more open to change in general and become a part of the active influencing process. Therefore, developing learning organizations is essential because the ability to change and influence dynamic systems will require greater shared knowledge than our organizations currently have (Senge, 1990). Organizational learning also affects ability to respond. If the organization shares information widely, individuals can choose to make daily adjustments without waiting to be told.

Organizations need to see their relationships with the external environ-ment as opportunities for mutual shaping, which require the identifica-tion of leverage points, which can trigger organic change. These kinds of leveraged interventions will be identified by the inverse relationship between the amount of energy it takes to implement the change and the scope of impact. Success will be achieved through continually assessing the effectiveness of our deep assumptions, letting go of ineffective ideas and behaviors, and adjusting intentions and behaviors accordingly.

Organizational Values: A network is a set of interdependent relationships. Therefore, the organization that embraces organic change values the time it takes to develop and maintain relationships. It sees decisions and actions as having implications beyond the specific component of decision-making. It values systemic thinking in employees so they understand the long-term implications of their choices. These organizations also value new ways of learning that help create generative knowledge for the community not just for the individual. Active learners, who teach their staffs to do the same and facilitate shared learning, are recognized as valued employees.

An organization that optimizes influence lets go of solutions which no longer work and looks at ways to redesign the present and future situation. The goal is to design a way out of a problem. For example, instead of thinking that freeway congestion is a problem of too many cars, one could look at current work and lifestyles. Technology creates leverage for changing our relationships to our office as well as time and distance. Being at work no longer necessarily means going to work. At the University of Southern California one of the financial officers for the student affairs division works from his home in Virginia.

Organizations that practice organic change would use new ways of leading that would leverage the connections of the system and the dynamics of interdependent networks to optimize the amount of influence it could have on the system. When we organize around optimizing influence, we value the ability to think systemically to gain wisdom about the dynamics of the system. Employees who can let go of the stability of the past and actively help shape the future would be valued.

There is evidence that student affairs staffs are playing with ways to optimize influence and intentionally shape the future. For example, the language of learning organizations and self-organizing teams is beginning to show up in our literature and conferences. Senior student affairs officers are exploring ways to design organizations to increase flexibility and many are being challenged to do business differently.

Meaning Making: Meaning in the organic change process is found through the ability to see connections and relationships between many variables. The system is considered a living entity rather than an inert mass. Therefore relationships are one way of understanding how the system might react to an intervention over time. Collective intelligence is an important asset for successfully influencing and shaping our environment because the complexity of the system cannot be understood through one person's eyes. It takes the combined perspectives of many individuals to understand the dynamics of the complex whole. In a networked system, change is as normal as breathing. Therefore, meaning is found in ongoing change rather than static assumptions. Ongoing innovation is a way of reflecting the natural dynamics of a networked system.

Why this Approach Works: When we organize around organic change strategies, we let go of control and optimize our ability to exert influence. We develop organizational structures that increase flexibility and find new ways of maintaining cohesion without traditional forms of control. A person who wants to impact an interdependent system needs the help of others. As others become actively involved, engaged, and responsible, the organization's ability to respond and intentionally shape the future increases. One of the keys to influencing a system is the realization that one person cannot do it alone! While we are still experimenting with these new forms of change, it is clear that their potential is great. There is still a lot to learn about triggering change organically. Our choice is to explore and learn a different way of interacting with our environment or live with the costs of ineffective change strategies.

Today, work demands different abilities and skills for different contexts. The organizing principles of control and stability were effective in times of great predictability. As the environment became more turbulent, the organizing principles of survival allowed us to react to the interruptions and surprises. However, as systems increasingly become more complex and dynamic, influencing the future becomes critical. We have the choice of mere survival (for a time) or learning to optimize our ability to influence the system in order to intentionally shape the future.

Images of Organic Change

We are all learners in using organic change strategies. When we are faced with learning something completely new, it is useful to use metaphors to help us play with new concepts. There are four analogies that reflect the dynamics of networked systems: 1) the relationship between force and resistance ("wet sand"); 2) the dynamics of fluctuations as harbingers of change ("birds on a wire"); 3) the role of leavening agents in change ("yeast"); and 4) how network connections can accelerate change (beneficial virus). The following images are analogs to these concepts. We invite you to look for your own organic examples in nature, technological systems, or the networked economy.

Wet Sand

As mentioned in Chapter One, wet sand demonstrates one of the properties of a networked system. It is made up of saline and silicone. When we forcefully put our foot down on wet sand, it congeals and our foot encounters a hard surface. However, when we gently place our foot in wet sand the sand slowly accepts our foot and allows our foot to sink into it. Wet sand operates like a network. It is made up of grains of sand and held together by saline. When it encounters force these elements combine to resist; however, when it encounters a slow entry into its system, it accepts the presence of the foreign object (our foot).

Human networks have a similar response to force. Anyone who has experience with crowd control at a spring college concert knows that a show of force can trigger a student riot. Like wet sand, when students encounter force, the elements of their human network combine and resist. However, when an intervention is infused slowly into the network, it accepts and adjusts to the intervention. The dynamic of how networks resist force is a natural aspect of any networked system. This is counterintuitive for those of us who have been trained in the "making change" "move swiftly and directly" school of hierarchical organizations. However, when we pause to reflect, we recognize the resistance that organizations demonstrate when positional power forces a direction on us without adequate time to understand or be involved in the change process. The next time you want to initiate change in your organization, think of wet sand. If we were to do this, we might provide more time for people to get used to the ideas we are suggesting, while also building extra time into the process to allow the system to respond to the ideas, reshaping them along the way.

Birds on a Wire

In the Midwest, we often see a flock of birds lined across telephone wires. If we were to pause in our work and watch the flock, we would see an interesting dance before they all left for their next destination. The dance generally follows a pattern. The birds sit on the wire and after a time, one or two birds take off. The birds that are left all flutter their wings but choose to stay in place. The birds that took off fly in a huge circle and eventually come back to sit on the wire with the rest of the flock. Time passes and again some birds take off, usually a few more following this time. Like before, the birds that remain on the wire all ruffle their wings when their fellow birds take off. Again, the birds that left circle back and land on the wire with their flock. This process of taking off and circling back continues with time delays in between action, and each time a few more birds follow and return. Eventually, when the birds take off, the entire flock lifts off with them, almost as if an unseen conductor was orchestrating them. The behaviors that initially look like failed attempts to get the flock moving actually are harbingers of a large-scale change for the whole flock.

This image of movement can also be seen in human organizations. Often individuals model a shift or change in the way they choose to do something. Each time there is a breaking of tradition, it causes a flutter in the rest of the organization. These experimenters often take off and return to the original way of doing things when they see they do not have support of their colleagues. However, if these individuals continue to experiment with change, each time they "take off" a few more colleagues go with them. Eventually, over time, the whole organization shifts. These dynamics of change are almost invisible to those of us trained in traditional forms of change. We have been taught that change is planned and then implemented. It is considered successful if the change is fully implemented the first time. In a networked system, change can occur over time triggered by creative individuals who model different ways of doing something. This process of fluctuations (a few birds taking off) repeated over time, eventually triggers large-scale change. The reason so many of us have missed this is because we are impatient. We believe that change should occur quickly. However, if we are patient and persistent we can be like those birds on a wire, triggering fluctuations that eventually shift the whole system.

Yeast

Bread baking is an organic process. However it requires a leavening agent for it to come into being. Yeast is often used as the active ingredient. In order to do its job, yeast has to be mixed with the proper ingredients and under the right conditions to become activated. This activation process requires the right temperature—not too hot, not too cold—and the right amount of sugar and water. Once the yeast is activated, it is mixed with dough. The dough and yeast with the right amount of kneading are placed in a warm place and given the time to interact. The dough is kneaded once more and set to rise again. Finally it is kneaded and placed into bread pans and baked in the oven.

Bread baking reminds us of the role of leavening agents in human systems. There are creative individuals in organizations who could be active agents and in combination with other people and under the right conditions, provide the leaven for change. Identifying these individuals and providing them with the right conditions to release their energy into the system is a key strategy to initiating innovation in a networked system. We often miss the importance of leavening agents in change because we are so fixated on the positional power in organizations. If we assume positional power is the leaven, we miss the wide number of people who could provide psychic, emotional, or other kinds of active ingredients required in any change process. We need to become more aware of the energy that individuals in organizations bring to a group or change effort. An organic change process needs active leavening agents.

A Beneficial Virus

We all are aware of how a flu or cold virus can spread. Invisible germs move with the aid of human contact to spread the flu. The flu virus actually uses the physical contact among humans to keep itself alive. While we do not want to spread a sickness through our organization, the dynamics of viruses can be instructional for understanding how things spread in a networked system. Any influencing process (or resistance process) in a networked system can spread quickly throughout the system depending on the quality of the network. An organizational grapevine is an example of how information can spread through a system. Once information is released into the system, it takes on a life of its own and the original message will be shaped and changed by members of the network.

Most of us are familiar with the negative side effects of rumors. They thrive on the dynamics of a networked system. The variety and quantity of the connections in the organization accelerate the speed of dissemination of rumor. Few of us can imagine a beneficial use of this dynamic; however, a network that can spread bad news can also spread good news. If we are to embrace the potential of organic change, we must also accept the nature of a network. The nature of a network is one of connection. These connections can accelerate the speed of information, rumor, or change in a system. While we cannot control the speed or accuracy of information in a system, we can amplify positive messages and dampen others (Eoyang, 1997). Instead of thinking only of the negative effects of a network and its "viruses," we need to learn to see the social, technical, and organizational connections of systems, and work with them to spread beneficial viruses.

The first three images of organic change invite us to see how natural or organic systems trigger change. They provide us with insights into how we might transfer and apply these dynamics to own ability to trigger change in our networked organizations. The last image of organic change helps us understand how the connections of the system will affect the rate of change. Depending on how networked the system is, the speed of innovation (or resistance) can be accelerated through its connections. Becoming more effective at organic change requires an appreciation of how a networked system works, a realization of what is controllable and what is not, and an ability to work in partnership with the dynamics of the system to facilitate change. Student affairs practitioners will find the underlying strategies of these four metaphors familiar, because we are expected to "control students' behavior." Since we know that students are not controllable, we have been forced to receive plenty of practice influencing the student culture in more organic ways. This experience can be transferred to influencing institutions and helping them learn how to practice organic change.

Optimizing Our Influence in an Interconnected World

We need to effectively respond to the way the dynamics of change are evolving. Engaging in organic change involves the ability to let go before we can intentionally influence the future of organizations. First, we need to let go of controlling strategies and optimize our influence in each situation we encounter. Control does not work in a networked system because the web-like relationships allow for flexibility and alternate routes to any destination. This flexibility means that control strategies will not cover all the possible variations or creative movement of the system. Second, we need to let go of the belief that we can change an organization on our own. A "Lone Ranger" strategy does not work in a networked system because multiple people must influence the system in order to intentionally shape a specific future. Networked systems respond to intentions, but not specific control. Third, we need to let go of the "I know all" mentality. Engaging in an organic process of change requires an organization to continually learn and innovate. A networked world is always in movement; it is easier to pace the movement of the larger system if the organization is also in movement. In contrast, if the organization is static, it takes a considerable amount of energy to get it moving to overcome inertia.

In order to increase our institutions' ability to respond to change in a way that helps us actively shape the future, we need organizations that have greater flexibility and can continually innovate in response to the external environment. The new role for student affairs is to become more conscious of organic influencing strategies and apply them to institution-wide issues. The following are some strategies for actively shaping the future through changing the way we think about organic change.

1. *Be open to the system.* Even if we wanted to, we could not close off or control the openness of the system. In an open system our value is related to our connection with the larger system, not to our isolation from it. Our job is to learn to be more open to the system, live in harmony with it, and teach others to do the same.

2. *Find diverse perspectives to help interpret what we see when we scan the external system.* Part of developing a new skill involves learning how to scan the larger environment so we can see patterns emerging from otherwise random events. There is always an underlying order in what may appear to be superficial chaos. However, a single individual cannot interpret the complexity of the system. The key to scanning the environment is to find other people who are also scanning the larger system and ask for their ideas, perspectives, and interpretations of what they see. It is through these dialogues that we begin to piece together a more complex and fuller understanding of what is emerging in the larger system.

3. *Hire people who have the ability to adapt to changing environments.* People have a variety of ways to respond to change. The need to hire employees who are open to change on both an individual and organizational level is important in this changing environment. People who actively resist change, like to control things, or maintain the status quo are not going to contribute to an organization's ability to change. We need to look for people who question their ways of doing things, their deep background assumptions, daily practices, and have a track record of adapting to changing circumstances. If we can model this ability to our students, they will also learn how to do this as well. This ability will help them in a world where inflexibility hinders success.

4. *Enhance the resilience of staff and organizations.* In times of rapid change greater levels of resilience on both individual and organizational levels are needed. Resilience is defined as the ability to recover quickly from change and resume a sense of balance after being bent, stretched or compressed. Conner (1995) states there are five characteristics of resilient people. First, they display a sense of security and assurance that is based in their ability to see opportunities where others see obstacles. Second, they have a sense of purpose. Third, they demonstrate pliability when confronted with uncertainty. Fourth, they develop multiple strategies to manage the ambiguity in their lives. Fifth, they engage in the process of change instead of defend against it.

5. *Learn upside-down thinking.* Handy (1989) states that discontinuous change requires discontinuous thinking. We need to develop the ability to think outside the box. Upside-down thinking makes connections where there are none, turns thinking on its side, and invites one to consider the absurd. Networks operate outside a linear structure, which makes upside-down thinking all the more necessary.

6. *Create a sunset law for all programs.* At times, the programs we create and implement can contribute to organizational inflexibility. We have developed such ownership and identity with these programs that we believe we need to keep them going. An interesting way to test how attached we have become to our programs (and the staff and resources needed to produce them) is to create a sunset law for all programs. A sunset law would give a three-year life cycle for each program before it is eliminated or a new variation takes its place.

7. *Find stability in order, not control.* The traditional view of stability is locked into a need for control. The assumption is that if we can control things enough, we can create stability. However, what if control and order is not the same thing? Organizations were originally designed to create orderly processes to help support the accomplishment of its goals. Over time, these organizing processes have become means of controlling people and their work. A world of innovation needs order, but does not thrive on control. We can benefit from using our roles as administrators to provide the support and structure that help individuals do their jobs—not control and therefore hinder their work.

8. *Reward experimentation and innovation, not perfection.* In a rapidly changing world, perfection is something that we might work on for many years, but which will not last long once achieved. Perfection requires a status quo world where standards of competence remain the same. Our staffs often measure themselves by their ability to be perfect. We think perfection is synonymous with competence. However in a world of innovation, we need to expand our level of experimentation. This does not fit well with a perfection mentality. When we increase informed experimentation, we expand innovation in our organizations.

The way things change is changing. We live in open systems that require us to engage in the process of organic change in order to actively influence and shape the future. Student affairs staff have the opportunity to create cultures that support openness and responsiveness to each other and the larger environment. Student affairs staff members need to learn to scan the external environment and use information to trigger individual and organizational change. In this networked world, *student affairs staff must actively help the rest of the institution engage in organic influencing strategies and learn to intentionally shape the external environment.* Control is not possible and survival is no longer enough. It is time to optimize our influence and intentionally shape our organizations through continual innovation in order to bring leadership of change to our divisions and institutions.

Reflective Questions:

1. How would structures, procedures, and management styles change if they were used to provide order rather than control people and productivity?
2. Are there different ways to design jobs to enhance flexibility and staffing patterns?
3. What aspects of our daily work are unpredictable?
4. How often and in what way am I surprised by what happens in my organization?
5. How can we teach creative upside-down thinking to professionals and graduate students?
6. How do we let go of linear concepts of change?
7. What is the role of leadership in helping organizations and staff cope with change and become perpetual innovators?
8. What kinds of organizing principles are helpful for living at the edge of chaos?

Chapter 4

New Ways of Learning

"In times of change learners inherit the earth, while the learned find themselves beautifully equipped for a world that no longer exists."
—Eric Hoffer

Marie kept asking her mother to stop for an ice cream cone. Finally her mom agreed to go to the ice cream shop. "Marie, what do you want?" her mom asked. Marie said, "A triple-decker cone." Her mom responded, "One scoop of ice cream would be more than sufficient." When Marie was given her cone, she looked at it and said, "Well, it may be sufficient but it certainly is not enough!"

Marie's response to her mother could apply as well to our educational approach at the advent of a knowledge era. In an industrial era, an instructional paradigm was sufficient, because it complemented the assembly line compartmentalized nature of organizations. A knowledge era accelerates the amount of new information and data that needs to be analyzed, processed, and synthesized. It also increases the amount of ongoing learning that is required over the course of both an individual's and an organization's life span. Given these different challenges, the current educational paradigm may be sufficient, but it is certainly not enough!

The background assumptions that have shaped the way we think about teaching in institutions of higher education reflect a traditional instructional paradigm. This is being challenged in part because of the changing external forces of a networked knowledge era. Barr and Tagg (1995) in their article, *From Teaching to Learning: A New Paradigm for Undergraduate Education,* describe the beginning of a shift from an instructional to learning paradigm. "In its briefest form, the paradigm that has governed our colleges is this: a college is an institution that exists to provide instruction. Subtly but profoundly, we are shifting to a new paradigm: a college is an institution that exists to produce learning. This shift changes everything" (p. 13). In this new paradigm of learning, the role of everyone in the university becomes oriented toward learning. This systemic orientation toward learning creates a new opportunity for all of us—students, faculty, and staff—to partner with each other and develop a new awareness of the learning process and generate knowledge of how to accelerate both individual and collective learning.

In a knowledge era, the academy cannot just be about instruction any more—it will be necessary to focus on a systemic approach to the generation of new knowledge. This systemic approach requires a broader definition of learning. The need for accelerated learning is a by-product of a networked world. Increased connectivity creates more movement in a system, which in turn, requires ongoing learning on both individual and organizational levels in order to continually adapt to the changing environment. In this chapter, we will offer

• an overview of a systemic approach to learning,
• a description of the nature of learning,
• an examination of the process of integrating learning,
• patterns of evidence of the paradigm shift, and
• a look at how individual intelligence can be transformed into collective intelligence.

A Systemic Approach to Learning

Our understanding of learning can be enhanced if we apply a systemic perspective to it. A system is the synergetic combination of all the parts, which form a complex whole. A systemic perspective is a point of view that can be used to more fully understand the many variables at play within a system and the interrelationships among them. This perspective requires organizational members to consider the whole as the primary lens of understanding instead of the parts. For example, when we bring a systemic perspective to the concepts of learning, we are able to gain insight into the set of interrelated ideas or developmental issues that form the complex whole involved in learning.

Understanding the process of learning from a systems perspective is becoming more important to both businesses and higher education. Developing learning organizations, which seek continuous improvement, is seen as essential for businesses to maintain a competitive edge. This concern for leveraging ongoing learning in organizations is a direct response to the challenges of a knowledge era. In recent years, themes have surfaced in the literature in higher education indicating growing support for a learning paradigm.

For example, *The Student Learning Imperative* (American College Personnel Association, 1994) articulates the important role that student affairs practitioners have in creating more powerful learning environments. The traditional language of instruction in higher education and identity of student affairs as only service providers is being challenged. The language of teaching and instruction is being supplanted by a learning paradigm, and in the process, higher education is being challenged to do more than transfer information from a "person who knows to a person who does not know." This language of learning brings a broader definition of what education is about and challenges us to search for new processes that support integrated learning (Kuh, 1996).

A systemic approach to learning has a variety of implications for higher education. *First, it challenges higher education to move beyond the perception that teaching is its central function.* Teaching can too easily be localized in a classroom and measured by the transference of knowledge from a faculty member to an individual student. A systemic approach shifts the locus of activity from teaching to learning, where students have greater responsibility for engagement in their learning processes.

The *second impact of a systemic approach to learning and knowledge generation is that others in the academy have an important role in extending and deepening the learning process, because learning can occur anywhere.* In today's global society learning is a daily occurrence involving many people, situations, and contexts. The learning environment in higher education is no different. However, we hinder our own ability to optimize the learning of students because we restrict the locus and responsibility of teaching to the classroom and faculty. We have many partners in our institutions that are interested and willing to help students integrate their learning. A systemic approach to learning would use these other resources.

The shift from an instructional paradigm to a learning paradigm mirrors the shift from an industrial to knowledge era. It is critical for higher education to engage in this shift in order to remain fully relevant and beneficial to society in a knowledge era. The need for this shift was demonstrated in a conversation with a group of alumni who have been in the workplace three to five years, in which they discussed the role and need for self-directed learning in their lives. They shared observations about their current jobs, which demand a faster pace of learning than their college experience. Another panel of human resource directors from five major Minnesota companies reinforced this message. All five members on this panel stated that an individual's ability to learn and to facilitate organizational learning is a standard expectation for their employees. They also stressed the importance of continually evolving as a learner and not becoming rigid in one's thinking.

The reality of today's work environment challenges higher education to become better at graduating individuals who can handle the self-directed nature and rapid pace of learning they will face in their future. This challenge involves accelerating the ability of individuals to take responsibility for their own learning and the collective learning of the organization. It also challenges individuals to integrate knowledge with practical know-how and experience. This kind of learning transforms knowledge and information into innovation and creativity.

We believe that in order to accomplish this kind of outcome for our students, a systemic perspective applied to the process of learning is essential. A systems view triggers different questions. How can we create a system where knowledge is generative on both an individual and organizational level? What are the components that need to be in relationship with each other in order for an individual to be a participant in a knowledge generating system? What are the components that need to be in relationship with each other in order for an organization to become a knowledge generating system? To address these questions, we need to start with observations of how learning occurs.

How Does Learning Occur?

We all can remember when we learned to ride a bike. The process of learning was motivated by our desire to learn, fueled by experimentation, risk, and mistakes, and supported by others' hints and encouragement. However, it did not always follow a logical course. It included learning detours in the form of bumps and bruises as well as that sense of exhilaration when we accomplished our first solo ride. Think of something you recently learned at work. How did you go about learning this new skill or knowledge? Did you initially identify the steps you would take before you began? In retrospect, did the actual learning process resemble your initial list? Much like the example of learning how to ride a bicycle, the reality of any learning process is rarely as neat as the original plan. Sometimes learning doubles back on itself, hits a dead end, and is filled with surprises, detours, and jumps forward. Learning in the classroom is often structured as a sequential event, but the learning process in its multiple contexts does not fit this linear path.

As an example we will look at a series of snapshots on how messy learning can be. Judy is a first year student at Everywhere University and she, like many of her peers, is learning about her values and how to apply them to her life.

Snapshot: Judy is enrolled in an ethics course. Her most immediate thought is—What do I need to do in this class to get an A?

Snapshot: Judy's roommate fell in love at orientation and now her boyfriend is spending many nights in their room.

Snapshot: Judy's new best friend in her history class asked Judy to share her answers on the first history exam. Judy felt uncomfortable but did not know how to say no.

Snapshot: Judy talked with the resident assistant (R.A.) about the situation with her roommate. The R.A. encouraged Judy to confront her roommate on her boyfriend's overnight visits. Judy talks to her roommate, but the conversation did not go well. She decided to cope in other ways. She made an appointment with the Resident Director to ask for a room change.

Snapshot: Judy had an insight in her ethics course that triggered a connection between her dilemmas in life and what she is learning about ethics.

Snapshot: Judy went to an assertiveness training workshop in order to learn how to stand up for her beliefs. She learned some new techniques that may help her more effectively confront her roommate. She decided to practice them with her friend who continues to ask her for help with history exams.

What we have described is nothing new. The process of learning does not remain bounded by the classroom or residence hall. Students' learning experiences are like a stream of events. Learning opportunities from a wide variety of contexts flow into one another without respect to the formal learning boundaries of an institution or set curricula. Yet, institutions often continue to compartmentalize students' learning processes. Given the seamless reality of how students actually learn, it seems that we, college administrators and faculty, continue to build dams that artificially obstruct the students' flow of learning. Student learning is not restricted to the classroom. In fact, learning will have the most profound impact when students see the application of concepts discussed in the classroom to their own lives. The goal for student affairs is to assist students in making these connections and to help the institution improve the overall quality of the learning environment.

Learning is Holistic and Difficult to Sequence

In Mary Catherine Bateson's (1994) book, *Peripheral Vision*, she describes learning as non-linear.

> *"[In] planning for the classroom, we sometimes present learning in linear sequences, which may be part of what makes classroom learning onerous: this concept must precede that, [or] be fully grasped before the next is presented. Learning outside the classroom is not like that. Lessons too complex to grasp in a single occurrence spiral past again and again, small examples gradually revealing greater and greater implications" (p. 30).*

In this sense, Bateson sees learning as a spiraling process where initial partial learning continues to spiral around allowing for fuller, more complete, understanding. In the first pass of a complex concept, one might grasp a part of it and still be puzzled by other aspects. These other aspects remain unclear and are stored in our peripheral vision for possible clarification at some later date. Over time, events and concepts stored in the peripheral vision of our minds come to make sense as we add new experiences and create more associations. "What we call the familiar is built up in layers to a structure known so deeply that it is taken for granted and virtually impossible to observe without the help of contrast" (p. 31). The classroom model has influenced the most familiar definition of learning; however, learning continues to occur in other contexts. In order to create integrated learning on college campuses, optimizing the learning that is occurring in these various contexts outside the classroom is critical. This kind of spiral learning process also describes how learning occurs in groups and organizations.

Many of the subject matters that are generally seen as part of the co-curriculum are very difficult to break down into some kind of linear sequence. In fact, every time we attempt to do so, it becomes a challenge because it does not fit into a sequential learning process. Multiculturalism, citizenship, group dynamics, leadership, and values clarification are just a few examples of content and skill areas that involve this kind of rich, complex and layered learning. One way to visualize this process is to imagine a marbled layered cake. Our learning has layers and patterns marbled throughout the cake. Like the double helix, the process of learning keeps spiraling through our lives, and with each encounter, there is an opportunity for deeper understanding, integration, and expansion of our learning. The snapshots of learning opportunities in Judy's first semester are typical of how events, knowledge, and skills interact to help her begin her journey of identifying and living her own values. This learning process of connecting theory, skills, and practice continues throughout Judy's life. The more Judy reflects on her life and makes connections between the classroom, her skills, and daily practices, the faster she will learn.

Learning is Non-linear

Another observation about learning is that students can get a profound insight and from that moment on their behavior changes. For Judy, the connection she made between her ethics course and her life dilemmas led to a behavior change. Triggering events that lead to learning might take place in the context of a conduct meeting or a counseling session. For others, it can take bumping their heads against a wall several times before they actually learn to change their behavior. We all have real life stories of students who visit ten years after they graduated to let you know that they finally got what everyone was trying to tell them while they were in college. The leaps and stalls of the learning process are natural. At times, our learning seems to plateau and stall out; while at other times we feel engaged in a learning thrill ride, holding on tight as we go through a series of 360-degree loops.

Just as individuals have leaps and stalls in their learning process, so do organizations. Many of us have experienced the frustration of meetings that seem to go nowhere and groups that continue to make the same mistake over and over again. This experience of learning how to create environments that support and foster diversity often resemble leaps and stalls. We also have experienced times when organizational learning has happened quickly and effectively—hospitals and public health offices are very effective at mobilizing effective community learning in response to an outside health threat.

Learning Requires Readiness

We know that an individual's awareness and readiness is key to whether an individual learns. For example, some students have to experience vast quantities of feedback before they understand there is something in their behavior that keeps getting them into trouble. These students behave as if they are irresponsible, but they appear irresponsible because they are not ready for learning to occur. All of us can think of times that we have received a great insight that radically changed the way we view things, perhaps through a book or a conversation with a mentor. Our perspectives were changed, in part, because we were ready to see things differently.

Organizational learning also requires readiness. Sometimes it takes an outside threat in order for an organization to put its creative minds to work. The threat triggers openness for learning. Organizational readiness can also be enhanced by a powerful vision or a meaningful set of core values. When an organization is asked to reflect on the difference between its current reality and its stated values, the awareness can trigger readiness for learning. If an organization does not see or believe in an outside threat, like the student example from above, it does not learn because it is not ready to learn.

Learning is Mutually Shaped by Individuals and Communities

As individuals learn, they influence the quality of the community learning. Conversely, the quality of the learning community helps individuals learn. Knowledge about ourselves often comes from our relationships within our communities. We begin to understand more fully who we are through others' perceptions of, and experiences with, us. What is created is a mutually shaping circle where individual learning shapes community learning, and community learning shapes individual learning. For example, as individual students living on campus, grow and develop they bring their new perspectives and capacities to the communities in which they live which, in turn, strengthens the quality of community on a residence hall floor. As communities evolve they also affect the learning and growth of individual students who are living within these communities. This cycle, in part, is one of the reasons why many colleges initially began with the concept of residential education. We intuitively understood that learning is a community event, not just an individual event.

Finally, the way learning occurs can be enhanced if we take the time to intentionally shape a culture for learning on campuses. Learning is at the very core of what higher education does. It is only when multiple individuals intentionally work toward a common shared purpose that the culture of learning on campuses can be reshaped. Using new ways of relating and influencing change are key strategies to facilitating this shift from an individualistic to a systemic approach toward learning. The point of leverage for an institution of higher education is to intentionally enhance the integration of learning on both individual and organizational levels. This kind of learning environment is vastly different from the fragmented educational system we have now.

Integrated Learning

Elements of Learning in a Networked Knowledge Era

What kind of system creates transformational knowledge? Learning in a networked knowledge era will need to be accelerated and shared. This implies that the way organizations function together will need to facilitate collective learning. Senge (1996) uses the term 'learning community' to describe the outcome an organization would have if it wanted to facilitate shared learning. He further identifies three elements of a learning community. The first element of a learning community is research or disciplined inquiry. *Disciplined inquiry* is a focused, intentional "approach to discovery and understanding [done] with the intent to share" (p. 1). The second element is capacity building. *Capacity building* occurs when we learn how to do something we did not previously know how to do. The third element is practice. "*Practice* is anything that people do to produce an outcome or result" (p. 1). Individuals who have achieved personal mastery continue to test, experiment, and apply their ongoing learning to what they currently know. They then use this ability to reflect in a manner that reshapes their conceptual understanding, capacity building, and practice. The difference between an average piano player and a professional pianist is the ability to continually integrate technique, theory, and a great deal of practice. The professional pianist models the integration of the three elements of a learning community.

Helen Astin (1996) is co-author of the *Social Change Model of Leadership*. Her disciplined inquiry into the theory of leadership extends beyond intellectual understanding and includes the real life experiences and capacities needed to implement this model. She is currently engaged in conversations with institutions that have adopted this model and is learning from their attempts to practice and implement it. These conversations take the form of grounded research, which in turn shapes her understanding of the Social Change Model and the capacities needed to achieve results on college campuses. These core elements—disciplined inquiry, capacity building, and practice—need to be integrated in order for innovative learning to take place. This generative learning occurs when intelligence gained from each element influences the other elements. By opening up the feedback loops between practice, disciplined inquiry, and capacity building, learning occurring in multiple arenas can be shared by the whole community. Generative learning is critical in situations where novel, complex problems are the norm. We need the integration of these elements to extend both our individual and shared learning for the challenges facing us today.

The Present View: Fractured Learning

Most colleges and universities have learning communities that are more fractured than integrated. When we separate the learning that occurs on campuses into different contexts—curricular, co-curricular, social, or work—we reinforce a fractured learning process. There is a cost associated with this separated learning. Students will continue to seek meaning and integration; however, it may not be the kind of integration that the college hopes to achieve. This process can be illustrated in the story of the flaming pumpkins.

Students were living in a theme residence hall, exploring issues of third world oppression. They were taking courses related to this topic and living together to extend the learning environment. One Halloween, six students were soaking toilet paper rolls in kerosene, stuffing them in hollow pumpkins, lighting them, and launching them out a third story window. A graduate student doing his dissertation on student culture was an observer of this activity. As he watched these pumpkins being launched out the window onto the street and sidewalk below, his past life as an assistant dean made it difficult for him to keep his mouth shut. He finally asked the students if they saw any relationship between this activity and the issues of oppression they were studying this semester. Were they becoming the oppressors of the housekeeping staff who would be required to clean up their mess tomorrow morning? The students paused in the midst of the third launch and, after a few minutes, acknowledged that he had a point. They repositioned the launch mechanism so the pumpkins instead would hit the grass across the street. The conclusion this researcher came to was that students will seek meaning, but it may not be the kind of integration that is fully possible.

Institutions need to work toward integrated learning, where learning from a variety of contexts can be brought into relationship with each other. The challenge of our institutions is to work toward this integration, not to reinforce the fractured learning model (Wingspread, 1993). Examples of how student affairs staff reinforce silos or fractured learning environments include keeping silent about or not being able to articulate the kinds of learning that occur in the co-curriculum and not being aware of the learning that students are experimenting with in their social lives. Student affairs staff can reinforce integrated learning in a variety of ways such as bringing staff, faculty, and students together to discuss common learning goals, asking questions that help trigger connections between life, work, and classroom concepts, and actively bringing knowledge about co-curricular learning into discussions at every level of the institution.

We also separate the learning occurring within each sector of the academy by creating infrastructures that limit feedback to and from the student population, faculty, and administrative staff. Very few institutions have a process for bringing members of the community together to discuss how the learning in separate contexts could support a common learning outcome. In higher education, disciplined inquirers are predominantly found in the faculty and their role is to impart their knowledge to students. Capacity builders are primarily found in student affairs and other staff members who see their role as helping students learn how to do things. Students in the academy are the practitioners, displaying their results to both the faculty and staff. These roles are descriptive and reflect the contexts in which we work. The fracturing occurs when the learning in one context is not brought into relationship with other contexts. A picture of this fractured learning community would look like Figure 4.1.

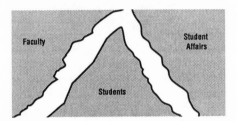

Figure 4.1: Traditional Fractured Learning Community

This version of the fractured academy does not allow feedback between the three core elements of the learning community. The faculty and staff do not exchange knowledge and insight with each other and the students' primary role is a passive receiver of knowledge and skills. Therefore, the learning and insights students gain in their practice is not continuously fed back to either the faculty or the student affairs staff. This lack of feedback throughout the academy isolates the learning process and keeps learning and integration (if it occurs at all) at an individual level. Like the larger society, each segment of the academy generates plenty of activity but the creation of generative knowledge for the community is inhibited.

New Ways of Learning

The Future View: Integrating Learning

A knowledge era challenges us to increase our knowledge about the learning process in order to accelerate learning on both an individual and organizational level. Creating an integrated learning process would require faculty, students, administrative and support staff to take the initiative to transfer and apply learning across contexts. We need to create intentional conversations with our students in order to enrich our own learning about capacity building, as well as the theories we are teaching in our classrooms. Likewise, we need to have closer ties between faculty and student affairs staff to see how we can complement each other's learning goals. An illustration of integrated learning is shown in Figure 4.2.

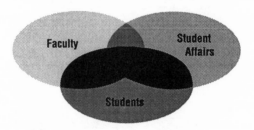

Figure 4.2: Integrated Learning

The integration of all three elements—disciplined inquiry, capacity building, and practice—actually requires a cast of thousands. Moreover, it requires faculty, staff, and students to come together to form a community that facilitates integrated learning (Kuh et. al., 1984). Student affairs staff can help bring this vision to the entire institution by practicing new ways of relating in their institutions. Through collaboration with others we can help people see how integrated learning can accelerate individual learning as well as expand our shared understanding of the learning process to the organizational level. An outcome of this kind of learning would be that everyone in the higher education community (faculty, staff, and students) would see how they contribute to students' learning and to the organization's ability to fulfill its mission. In achieving this goal, the academy would be modeling for students a critical competency required for the knowledge era.

If faculty and student affairs staff were to work together to facilitate learning, we can make some educated guesses as to how it might look. Faculty would bring their focus on disciplined inquiry into relationship with student affairs' orientation on capacity building. They would work together to create linkages and knowledge related to how they were both contributing to helping students practice and integrate knowledge and capacity. In addition they would have conversations with each other to assess the quality of learning that was occurring and reflect on ways to improve the learning process. This kind of integration of theory and skills is not foreign to faculty who teach in the performing arts. The theater department, for example, mixes the disciplined inquiry of theater with capacities and practice as a natural part of their approach to teaching. Transferring this approach to the rest of campus would dramatically enhance students' ability to integrate their learning. Other pockets of this approach to learning are evident in the adoption of service learning pedagogy and the way business departments are reaching out to form strategic partnerships with corporations.

Influencing the creation of integrated learning may seem like an overwhelming task—especially if all one currently sees is fragmentation and turf wars on one's campus. Thoughts like "this is too far out there," "this is too complicated," and "this sure would not work at my institution" would be a sampling of responses. However early indications, if we knew how to look for them, might tell us a different story about our institution's overall readiness for these ideas.

Signs of Readiness for Integrated Learning

Usually we look for change in institutional mission, vision statements, presidential speeches, and strategic plans. We wait for these visible articulations before we believe that our institution is ready for change. However, there is another way to look for signs of readiness. Transformational change usually starts in pockets of our institutions before it breaks the surface of organizational consciousness. This process resembles the birds on a wire metaphor from Chapter Three. Organizational fluctuations are created as various iterations of integrated learning are created in an institution. Eventually, like the birds who finally take off en masse, the organization transforms itself into a community that fosters integrated learning.

Organizational Patterns of Evidence

There are many examples of organizations that are experimenting with integrated learning processes. For example, the student affairs staff, in collaboration with students and faculty at the University of Southern California, have created an electronic portfolio to facilitate integrated learning. The portfolio is designed as a self-directed learning tool. First, it allows students to access information about opportunities available at the university. Examples include information about academic majors, student leadership opportunities, volunteer experiences, research opportunities, student internships, and employment opportunities. Second, it outlines learning expectations that the university has of its students and corresponding strategies to meet these learning goals. Third, it allows students to keep a personal diary of their experiences and is designed to foster students' integration of their learning experiences. Through this kind of integration they have a greater understanding and awareness of the connections between their academic, co-curricular, and personal experiences at college.

This approach to self-directed learning has important implications for student affairs and higher education in general. First, it is a systemic intervention in the learning culture of the student. By inviting the student to be in charge of recording and making connections between different aspects of college, it models the kind of self-directed learning that will be expected in their future. Second, it suggests that a learning environment can be designed in such a way that allows for learning without direct one-on-one faculty or staff contact. Therefore, the impact on student learning can be vastly extended, yet still be personalized. Third, the electronic portfolio provides an infrastructure to faculty, students, and staff that supports a form of integrated learning. Finally, it exemplifies how a student affairs staff can creatively initiate a way of actualizing the mission statement of the university, making a vision of integrated learning part of it.

The service-learning movement is more evidence that integrated learning is occurring on many campuses. It is a wonderful example of a pedagogy that reflects the idea behind integrated learning. The combination of theory with meaningful service activities, followed by critical reflection, brings disciplined inquiry into relationship with the capacity building and practice opportunities embedded in the service experience. The power of this form of learning is in part why the movement has such passionate supporters.

We can also learn from the Motorola Corporation, a global communications company based in Chicago. They are engaged in

> *"an ambitious transformation program intended to embrace every employee in the company. Core company values, valued traditions of leadership, and the fundamental human skills required to make the company prosper are all being reinvented. New learning skills are being*

instilled through huge investment in learning research. Company educa-
tion programs and learning skills are being exported into the community
and the local school system in an effort to retrain tomorrow's employees,
customers, and suppliers" (Zohar, 1997, p. 3).

Needless to say, this does not reflect short-term thinking.

These signs of readiness all have unique histories of how they came into being. Some of them have taken advantage of national movements that are applied to local campuses. Others used opportunities that emerged locally to extend a vision of an integrated learning environment. Still others have grown through grassroots conversations about the deep values and passions individuals have about their work. All of these patterns of evidence have taken time to become visible on our campuses. This kind of change needs to be viewed as a long-term journey rather than an annual goal or part of a three-year plan. In order to have a long-term view of change, student affairs staff will need to believe "in their gut" that this holistic approach to student learning and institutional transformation is worth the time it takes to get there. We will have to confront our own beliefs about learning and the value of integrated learning. One of the key questions for student affairs is whether we can coalesce around learning as an overarching value of higher education (Allen & Garb, 1993). Our future as a profession resides in the co-creation of integrated learning resulting in the acceleration of both individual and organizational learning.

Transforming Individual Intelligence into Collective Intelligence

Student affairs professionals need to take responsibility for and provide leadership in helping institutions respond to the challenges of a knowledge era. This will require us to facilitate seamless learning experiences and break down the false boundaries between faculty and student affairs. In Chapter Two, we suggest that student affairs staff begin to influence their organizations to think and practice new ways of relating. In Chapter Three, we advocate that student affairs staff influence change organically. Now we encourage student affairs staff to use those relationships and change strategies to introduce shared learning processes to facilitate integrated learning among students, faculty, and staff.

The following practices can help transform individual intelligences into a collective intelligence. When we create shared learning on an organizational level, we help institutions generate new knowledge and adapt to the challenges of a networked knowledge era. At the same time, if institutions model these collective learning processes, we help students learn how to facilitate organizational learning as well.

1. *Shift from a fragmented to a networked lens.* We need to relinquish our territorial perspective and see ourselves as part of a network. When we shift our orientation, we become open to others' perspectives and how they can be combined with our perspectives to create greater institutional learning.

2. *Become learning focused.* What would happen if every task and service were done with the intent to maximize individual/organizational learning or integrated learning? Would our response to roommate conflicts or student employment be any different? If we connected what we were modeling for our students to the kind of citizens we hoped they would become, what would change about our behavior? When we become learning focused, we begin to ask these and other questions. We look at what we are responsible for doing and see how it can reinforce the learning goals of institutions or society's expectation of what a citizen of the future will need to learn in order to become a productive member of society.

3. *Create partners in learning.* Actively integrating our community so that generative knowledge can be created individually and organizationally requires all of us to see ourselves in partnership with each other in the creation of learning environments. We need to believe that integrated learning is our primary work. We need to have conversations and retreats with our staffs on what this means on our particular campus and how we can see ourselves as learners within a division of people committed to optimizing learning. This divisional commitment to learning is one of the steps that help student affairs staffs come to the table with faculty and students as partners in learning. Student affairs practitioners need to use facilitation skills to create ways for students to engage in this partnership as well.

4. *Take small steps and big steps simultaneously.* The small steps we need to take with students are to help them see connections in their learning. The small steps we can take are to have our staff ask students "what they learned today" and concurrently ask themselves, "what did you learn today?" The big steps we need to take with faculty, students, and staff are developing the learning outcomes to which we as a community will commit. Further, we need to orchestrate ongoing dialogues with others on how to design more effective self-directed learning structures. These big and small steps are taken with the intent to facilitate movement towards integrated learning.

5. *Become the designers of integrated learning processes.* Leaders in learning organizations design the structure and environment that support the organizational outcomes. Senge (1996) tells a story of asking leaders which role they believed is most important on an ocean liner. Many suggest that the captain is the primary role. Senge countered that designers of ships are most relevant, because they create the design and maneuverability. Student affairs staff need to see themselves as designers of community learning processes.

6. *Model active integrated learning.* We need to model integrated learning on three levels: individual, divisional, and institutional. If we become more integrated in the way we individually learn, we become models of a more integrated approach to learning. This modeling can help others learn how to become integrated learners. Further, divisions of student affairs need to model integrated learning in order for the larger institution to see this concept in practice. If we can encourage and facilitate the dialogues that result in our institution's ability to model this kind of learning community, we impact our students in powerful ways.

Student affairs professionals have a responsibility to *help higher education move from an instructional to a learning paradigm.* This work will help institutions remain relevant in a networked knowledge era. It will also increase students' ability to be prepared for and contribute to the future. Our leadership role is to actively introduce shared learning processes into our institutions. We never said this would be easy!

Reflective Questions:

1. How well do you individually integrate disciplined inquiry, capacity building, and practice?
2. How well does your department, division, and institution model integrated learning?
3. What percentage of your student affairs division believes that learning is a central role for them?
4. What professional development activities could help your division initiate dialogue about the impact they have on students' learning and their learning environment?
5. Who are the individuals you know who create "knowledge generating systems?"
6. What programs on your campus integrate disciplined inquiry, capacity building, and practice?
7. How do we get students to their own thresholds of readiness for real learning?
8. What steps could you take to promote integrated learning on your campus?

Chapter 5

New Ways of Leading

"We are now entering an Age of Unreason, when the future in so many areas, is there to be shaped, by us and for us—a time when the only prediction that will hold true is that no prediction will hold true; a time, therefore, for bold imaginings in private life as well as public, for thinking the unlikely and doing the unreasonable."

—Charles Handy

How do we create an organization that has both the flexibility and durability needed in this complex, rapidly changing world in which we live? This is the question that many people in higher education, businesses, and non-profit organizations are struggling with today. Each week a new book is released providing another model of how to lead or structure organizations in order to increase the ability to react more effectively to the changes being presented. Some books recommend becoming a learning organization, others suggest total quality improvement, and still others advocate re-engineering. Others recommend redesigning organizations and emergent leadership concepts in order to lead a networked organization (Heenan & Bennis, 1999; Matusak, 1997; Morgan, 1997). Through our reading and daily practice in each of our growing networked organizations, the authors have drawn from a variety of these concepts to create a new synthesis involving four new ways of working, which when applied to organizations, can create both effective and flexible environments to adapt to change.

We have thus far examined the importance of relationships in networked systems, organic change strategies that require us to see and understand the system to influence change, and the need for a systemic perspective to assist in the development of integrated learning. In a networked world, one must also practice a systemic perspective for effec-

New Ways of Leading

tive leadership. Learning how to lead organic systems is essential if we want to actively shape the future. This chapter will describe new ways of leading in today's networked organizations, including using systemic thinking, developing new forms of organizational cohesion, and weaving new ways of relating, influencing change, and learning into the practice of leadership. Individuals who can learn how to do this will have indispensable gifts and talents they can give to their organizations.

Systemic Thinking: Seeing Connections

New ways of leading require the ability to think systemically. One cannot make sense of relationships and connections by looking at a small part of the system. Relationships and connections need to be viewed holistically. Holistic thinking is not new to our practice. Student affairs philosophy is founded on a holistic approach to students' development (National Association of Student Personnel Administrators, 1989). Student personnel work has always included the social, emotional, cognitive, moral, spiritual, and physical aspects of an individual. This multi-faceted look at an individual's growth has been termed holistic development. As practitioners, we are predisposed to viewing students this way, by looking for the connections between emotional and cognitive development. What is already natural for us with an individual can be applied to understanding organizational systems. These connections are the way we recognize the interdependent relationships in our organizations. Holistic thinking is similar to systems thinking except it is applied at a different level. If holistic thinking helps us to understand the interconnectedness of the individual student, systems thinking helps us to understand the interconnections between the individual, other human beings, the organization, and the environment.

One way of expanding our thinking to the organizational level is to become aware of our "blind spots." Barry Oshry (1995) identifies four types of blindness that hinder individuals' ability to think systemically: spatial blindness, temporal blindness, relational blindness, and process blindness. "When we don't see systems, we fall out of the possibility of partnership with one another.... All of this happens without awareness or choice" (p. xii). If we can bring consciousness and choice to our work by taking our "blinders" off, we can begin to engage with others in more constructive ways that serve the larger purpose of our organization and society. We identify two forms of perspectives that hinder our awareness of system dynamics. They are spatial and inter-relational awareness.

Spatial Awareness

Spatial awareness brings a consciousness to the way space affects perceptions of the organization and how time—past, present, and future— interact to constrain or facilitate work. One aspect of spatial awareness is the capacity to see the whole system. When individuals lack this awareness, they see what is happening in their part of the organization but do not understand what is happening elsewhere. As a result they have difficulty seeing the organization as a whole. For example, Sue worked for a state university as the Director of the Student Union. One fall, she was frustrated by the detailed request from the State University Board Office to generate a ten-year repair and replacement list in the next three weeks. Her irritation was enhanced by the fact that she had a lot of things currently on her plate, including student staff training, orienting a new assistant director, homecoming, and general start-up of a new year. While Sue was very aware of what life was like for her, she was not aware of what life was like for the State University Board Office. She thought that Juan, who made the request, was being difficult and possibly incompetent. "Doesn't he know what I am dealing with?" On the other hand, Juan had been put in charge of developing information for a hearing on a long-term repair and replacement-funding bill with the higher education committee of the state legislature. Needless to say, Juan had his own pressures. In fact, he was wondering if Sue was incompetent: "Doesn't she see how important this is? Why is it taking her so long to respond?"

This situation or some variation occurs every time another office asks for our cooperation without understanding our issues, stresses, and dilemmas. If we cannot see past our part of the organization, misunderstanding and conflict can occur. Once we see the whole picture we understand why others are requesting our help. In addition to seeing our own issues we begin to understand their issues, stresses and any underlying emotions that are affecting the situation. When we work in a system that is spatially aware, we understand each other's work and what the organization is doing as a whole. As a result, respect, empathy, and cooperation increase in the organization and the amount of conflict and territorial behavior decrease.

The second aspect of spatial awareness involves our sense of time. When we lack this awareness, we disconnect what is happening in the present from the past and the future. When we are unaware of time, we understand the situation we are in currently, but we do not understand how our past behaviors or context have led us to this point or how our current behavior will affect our future. In this sense, we are oblivious to our history in the same way we may be unaware of the other parts of the organization.

For example, Mike is often struck by how the history in his organization affects what is possible today. He is a director of a performing arts program, which was in the red when he was hired. Before this time, the program had usually made money. However, since that one year in the red, the comptroller has been watching over every decision. Mike, unlike many individuals, is aware of how history affects his current situation. However, he also needs to be aware of the "historical" impact of the present. The way he responds to the comptroller today will affect his department's future. In other words, the way he solves today's problems will affect the kinds of problems he has in the future.

Inter-Relational Awareness

Inter-relational awareness brings a consciousness to the ways we connect to each other and the patterns that evolve in the common processes of our working relationships. Inter-relational awareness examines how positions, and the common ways we do things, can help or hinder the quality of our work. For instance, in Jose's position as director of counseling, he feels the burden of responsibility for achieving the goals of the department. His staff lets him assume as much control as he needs but does not actively support him. He thinks he is holding the center together, while his staff feels oppressed. They are caught in a "destructive dance." An outside consultant helped them all see how their behaviors were affecting the quality of their relationships. Now Jose is allowing more decisions to be made by the center staff. The staff members are more conscious of their roles and how they affect the relationships and dynamics of the group. They all are beginning to make active choices toward true partnerships.

Inter-relational awareness calls us to become conscious of the dynamics of the whole system. Often we see individuals within a system, but do not see the whole system. An example of becoming aware of process patterns is found in a "quick-fix archetype" (Senge et.al., 1994). A metaphorical example of the quick fix archetype is a squeaky wheel. If we had a squeaky wheel on a child's wagon and threw water on it, the noise would initially disappear. However, it would come back, and this time it would be louder. Since water worked last time, we would throw water on it again—however, the noise would continue to reappear over and over again unless we stopped to look at our assumptions about the process we were using to solve this problem. When we stop and reflect, we might discover that oil would actually solve the problem of the squeaky wheel better than water. Even the oil will not work forever! If we were oblivious to the process, we would not stop and examine why our behavior was not working. Learning to recognize the processes of the whole is an important tool in a networked world.

An aphorism that applies is this: if it happens a first time it is an accident; if it happens a second time it is a coincidence; if it happens a third time it is a pattern; and if it happens a fourth time it is deliberate. How many of us have been in a situation where the same mistake occurs over and over again, only to become a deliberate way of operating, no matter how inefficient? Spatial awareness and inter-relational awareness help us discern the myriad of connections and relationships that currently exist in our organizations. Thinking systemically is critical in networked organizations because of their dynamic nature. One cannot develop an overall understanding of them without a systemic perspective. Networked organizations are fundamentally uncontrollable, which requires that we find new forms of creating organizational cohesion.

New Forms of Organizational Cohesion

In hierarchical organizations, there are sets of traditional variables we use to maintain order. Many of these traditional variables are designed to ensure control. Goals are attached to performance appraisals and performance appraisals are attached to reward systems such as salaries and promotions. The standardization of policies and procedures is designed to create uniformity, predictability, and fairness. Policies are written in such a way to try to encompass all the interesting variations that humans can present to them.

However, policies will never actually encompass all the different situations that students present to us. Goals will never actually predict all the important things that we need to do. Performance appraisal systems will never actually assess all the intangible things we care about. While these traditional organizational variables have their uses, they are not enough to maintain cohesion in a networked knowledge based organization.

How does one maintain order in a networked organization? Control can hinder effectiveness in a networked organization, so what can take the place of the familiar vehicles we use to control organizational functioning? Networked organizations shift the focus on control to organizational cohesion. There are emergent constructs that can help maintain a sense of order and cohesion in an organization. These emergent ideas reflect the organic nature of a human system and can either work along side more traditional tools or can take their place. These are core values, strange attractors, fractals, optimizing tensions, and using fluctuations as triggers for change.

Core Values

Wheatley (1995) talks about the importance of core values as an aspect of our identity. Zohar (1997) believes that deep transformation is only triggered through deeply held core values and the passion or commitment that they generate. Our core values, the things that we truly care about, can shape our work and our behavior in powerful ways. When an individual's values match the organization's values, a natural alignment between the individual and organization occurs. If organizational values are disconnected from or at odds with an individual's core values, a state of nonalignment is created. This results in a low sense of cohesion within the organization. Core values allow organizations to achieve adherence to a common direction while providing the degree of individual freedom needed to manage the complexity of these organizations (Halal, 1998).

Strange Attractors

Another emergent notion that can help maintain cohesion comes from the science of chaos. The science of chaos studies non-linear dynamic systems. Human behavior reflects the characteristics of this kind of system. Despite the surface chaos and seeming disorder in non-linear dynamic systems, there is an underlying order to the randomness. In chaos theory, scientists found that strange attractors defined the outer boundary within which the system behavior operates (Glieck, 1987; Wheatley, 1992). There are usually a variety of strange attractors in a natural system; their interplay dynamically defines the range of behaviors that exist within the system. In a human system, core values can sometimes act as strange attractors and, like an invisible force field such as gravity, shape the actions of individuals. For instance, values often act as strange attractors in our lives. The values parents impart to their children actually create a boundary within which children experiment. When sons and daughters come to college, they continue to experiment; however, their choices are bounded by their values.

The concept of strange attractors holds a key for organizing institutions without the need for traditional control mechanisms. For example, questions worth asking can be used as a form of a strange attractor. By asking deep questions, employees begin to pay attention to their behaviors with others. This, in turn, creates a greater awareness of their own behavior over time. The strategy of asking a question that has no easy answer and keeping the question in front of employees shifts the behavior of an organization without a formal change effort. For example, Kathy posed the question, "are we challenging our students enough?" Her concern was that, while her staff was very good at supporting and encouraging students, they were not equally comfortable with challenging their students. Through asking this question, the staff began to pay attention to their behaviors with students. This, in turn, created a greater awareness of their own behavior over time. These questions were worth asking, and the energy generated by keeping them in front of the staff shifted the behavior of the student affairs division.

A meaningful vision can also act as a strange attractor in an organization. The vision becomes the attractor that people organize around. If the vision is clear and meaningful, individuals in an organization will use it to influence their daily choices. Because strange attractors define the outer boundary of a system, the vision can be a powerful way to create organizational cohesion.

Fractals

Chaos theory states that fractals are another form of order in an organic system. A fractal is a pattern that repeats itself on different scales (Gleick, 1987; Wheatley, 1992). It can be a very simple operating rule that allows for infinite variation in the universe. For example, if a tree has an operating rule in its DNA that states that every branch on the tree would have two additional branches of equal length, the tree would eventually take on a symmetrical form that we sometimes see in nature, like the shape of an umbrella. (See Figure 5.1)

Figure 5.1: Symmetrical Tree

However, if the tree has a different DNA operating rule, a different shape would occur. If every branch that is formed on a tree had two branches of unequal length that grew out of each limb, than it would take on an asymmetrical form. (See Figure 5.2)

Figure 5.2: Asymmetrical Tree

The beauty of a fractal is that it allows natural growth to occur, and yet is bounded by a simple operating rule tucked in the DNA. In trees, the fractal can be seen on both a large and small scale. On each branch, the rule of equal or unequal length applies, and each succeeding branch will create a similar replicating pattern as it grows.

In human organizations, we also have fractals that we grow and observe. We have human fractals that occur in our larger society that take root in our local campuses. For example, in the 1960's the social action movement happening nationally showed up on many of our campuses; sometimes it was initiated locally—a "small scale fractal";— sometimes it grew out of a national focus—a "large scale fractal." We can see both good and bad fractals, currently growing throughout the country. For example, cynicism about government in our society is also being applied to student senates on campus. This is a national fractal that is being repeated locally.

Positive fractals can be nurtured and grown in an organization. For example, if we operate with integrity and authenticity with students, they, in turn, may respond in kind. When a student affairs staff member says he or she is going to plant a seed of an idea with a student group, this is a variation of growing a fractal. The seed is like the operating rule in the tree's DNA. In a human system, an operating rule can take the form of a concept or idea.

A fractal can be grown on a departmental basis as well. Departments whose members embed learning into every aspect of their organization are growing a fractal that will help them become a learning organization. This fractal (in the form of an idea) can spread to other individuals and departments like the beneficial virus metaphor of organic change. Fractals are another way to build order and unity in an organic organization.

Optimizing Tensions between Opposites

Another emergent variable for organic systems is the concept of tensions. In a binary thinking process, the value of something has to be either zero or a one. Often we use an either-or thinking in organizations. We act as if there is either a right answer or a wrong answer. When we align with others of like minds, fragmentation can occur within an organization. In organic organizations, however, the tensions between opposites are a natural state and indicate a healthy organization. For example, change and stability are opposites that are healthy to have in an organization because too much of one without the other can lead either to chaos or decay. In a networked organization, having a healthy tension between opposites can lead to growth, learning, and evolution. We are familiar with this notion of tension in student affairs. For instance, we optimize both challenge and support to trigger students' development. The notion of optimizing tensions exists in other areas as well. The tensions between boredom and anxiety can elicit learning. With each of these opposites, holding the tension between things can trigger growth.

When we invite both stability and change to peacefully co-exist in an organization, we end up with "stable instability" (Stacy, 1992). If we were trying to balance the tension between control and chaos, we might find that the place where both meet is the nexus of flexibility and order. This kind of tension naturally exists in organic systems. Accepting and inviting tension into organizations is a different way of thinking about how organizations evolve. By resisting the urge to dichotomize issues, we can begin to play with the relationship between opposites. This opens ourselves and others to the possibility that an organization may need both of the opposite values and ideas to continue to evolve and innovate. For example, integrating diversity and maintaining tradition often appear to be mutually exclusive. When we optimize the tensions between them we become open to ways of enriching traditions and diversity simultaneously. Developing the personal and organizational capacity to allow opposites to peacefully co-exist is an essential skill in complex organizations. Strangely enough, optimizing tensions between opposites also provides organizational cohesion.

Fluctuations as a Sign of Transformation

The final emergent variable for organic organizations described in this chapter is seeing change as an organic process. When an organization goes through transformation and change, there are indications of this evolution in fluctuations from the status quo. When fluctuations occur initially, it is a way for the system to experiment with new ideas. Our traditional view suggests that change is a controlled, linear and planned event. In an organic organization, change strategies revolve around the encouragement of experimentation and fluctuations that are tested over time. Sometimes the fluctuation is dampened down by the system and then crops up in another iteration. These repeated fluctuations and variations of change, over time, become perceived as more relevant and important to the future of the organization. At this point, the ideas begin to be formally tested and encouraged in the formal system. In an organic system, we always have an informal and almost unconscious element of change occurring. This process works like waves in the ocean. At the point where one wave is at its peak, ready to crash down, there is always another wave forming underneath. Organic systems always have a new wave forming underneath the current one. The trick is to look for the next wave at the same time we are riding the current wave (Lynch & Kordis, 1988).

Usually we see fluctuations as signs of instability. In an organic system, fluctuation is a sign of a living healthy system. This principle is exemplified in nature. Otters only settle in areas with running water. They know that movement is a sign of a healthy environment. When we use planned and controlled change as a variable of cohesion, we actually are in conflict with the natural change process of the organization's system. Instead, we need to see fluctuations as forms of dynamic cohesion and nurture them in our system.

These emergent variables of core values, strange attractors, fractals, optimizing tensions, and fluctuations of change all become ways to bring cohesion and order to an organic system. We need to start paying attention to and nurturing these variables in organizations. As we make these forms of order stronger in organizations, we actually increase the freedom of individual behavior. These new organizational variables become important in our ability to learn how to lead organic systems. The traditional and emergent variables are summarized in Table 5.1.

Traditional and Emergent Forms of Cohesion

Traditional Forms	Emergent Forms
Goals	Core values
Performance appraisals	Strange attractors
Procedures and policies	Fractals
Either-or thinking	Optimizing tension between opposites
Planned change	Fluctuations as a sign of transformation

Table 5.1

Although these emergent variables may seem strange at first, we have been using them intuitively in student affairs. Take, for example, the issue of alcohol use on campuses. This is one of those challenges that defy the traditional variables of a mechanistic organization. While we are not in control of our students, we do seek to influence their behavior. Students have minds of their own and the peer culture of the student body exhibits the characteristics of a networked system. We have used policies, goal setting, planned change, and either-or thinking and still are a long way from healthy choices on campuses. Policies get revised on alcohol use, and we set goals on the number of alcohol education programs or alcohol free events we sponsor each year. Sometimes we seek solutions by forcing choices between alcohol-free Greek rushes or setting standards of zero tolerance for alcohol-related discipline cases.

These attempts help us feel like we are "doing something" to combat binge drinking and the negative consequences of this behavior. We know, however, that these strategies are not enough. Intuitively we have been experimenting with alternative strategies. Many health educators have realized that more holistic and creative strategies are needed. If we were to overlay the emergent variables onto some of these creative initiatives, we would see some familiar strategies.

Some campuses have reinforced core values such as personal integrity, respecting yourself, respect for others, and even moderation to trigger more effective personal choices. Other campuses have used service activities or involvement as strange attractors in the student body. The assumption is that if students are attracted to positive activities, they will experience a deeper sense of connection and community and be less attracted to the false sense of community experienced at alcohol-related parties. We are experimenting with developing fractals when we set up healthy living communities in residence halls or when certain national fraternities determine that all of their chapters will be alcohol free within three years. These choices support alternative living environments that are growing over time. A healthy fractal that starts small can spread to the larger campus culture. We have also used tensions to trigger behavior change. Peer marketing of the actual amount of alcohol students drink provides intellectual tension to the assumption that "every one drinks on our campus, so why not me?" Holding the line on discipline cases involving alcohol can also use the resulting tension as a teachable moment with a group or individual. Each of these strategies triggers fluctuations in the environment. When these fluctuations persist, the culture eventually is changed. We have learned that one perfect solution does not exist. The interdependent nature of the abuse of alcohol requires a family of solutions working in coordination with each other. Using the emergent variables in relationship to each other is a powerful way of increasing the cohesion of an organizational strategic response.

Weaving New Ways into the Practice of Leadership

Leadership in an organic system requires a shift in focus. Leadership in an emergent paradigm organizes around

• meaning making,
• facilitating the flow of energy,
• organizational renewal (using new ways of relating and influencing change),
• facilitating organizational learning, and
• developing the capacities of others.

Meaning Making

A very important focus for leadership in a networked knowledge system is meaning making—the ongoing process of helping people see the connection between their day-to-day work and a shared sense of purpose. Given the dynamic movement and constant change, meaning provides organizational ballast. In a sailboat, ballast is a term that describes the way weight is distributed in the boat's design. When a sailboat has proper ballast, it has balance built into its design. Ballast makes it hard to tip over and, if it does turn over, easy to right again. The creation of meaning is the attempt to give ballast to a networked organization, and it is a never-ending process of change. Meaning making in organizations and individuals is a journey, not a destination. The goal of meaning making is to connect daily actions to something larger and thereby provide a sense of purpose to our work. New ways of leading facilitate the development of this shared organizational "space of significance" where a sense of greater meaning can be nurtured.

Facilitating the Flow of Energy

Traditional management has influenced our ideas of leadership. Traditional leadership assumes that we work in the tangible realm of the system, like production, products, and resources both human and material. In an organic system, the leadership focus shifts from the tangible to intangibles—toward fields of energy. Field theory helps us to see how vision could be a field of energy around which the organization forms. Energy in an organic system is a very important resource for our organizations. Energy needs to be recycled in order to continue to renew the system. Activities need to generate energy rather than consume it. When we bring people together, we need to be conscious of how energy flows at a meeting. If there is less energy at the end of the meeting than there was at the beginning, something is wrong in the energy field. Leaders in an organic system look for ways to bring people together, design programs, and encourage others to generate energy.

In thermodynamics, we study how unorganized energy becomes focused and turned into "work." Work in this context is the way we use unorganized energy. The second law of thermodynamics examines the loss of energy when the shift from unorganized energy to work occurs. The efficiency of this shift is measured by the relationship between the total amount of energy available and the work that is accomplished. Many organizations today consume an inordinate amount of human and material energy generating a product. In a networked knowledge era, we need to experiment with new organizational structures and processes that diminish the amount of wasted energy. For example, if we work from this frame, our focus would shift from obstacles and overcoming resistance to opportunities and attracting energy to a change event. Becoming aware of human energy and its flow, in particular its losses, is the first step to this aspect of a new way of leading.

Organizational Renewal: Using New Ways of Relating and Influencing Change

Another important leadership process in organic systems is triggering change using the natural dynamics of the system. The community college president described in Chapter Two is changing peoples' view of the college and their ways of doing business. Initially, he brought in emergent thinkers to generate new ideas. As a result of these conversations an insight emerged that suggested good group facilitation could accelerate and augment organizational renewal. As a result, facilitation training was made available to all members of the institution. Over time, this strategy created a shift in the way the organization operated. By interjecting good facilitation skills at all levels, many of the meetings that naturally occurred on his campus were impacted. As a result, new relationships were formed, information was shared broadly, and organizational learning occurred. This, in turn, renewed the system. His focus was on renewal, not on production. He believed that productivity would occur as long as renewal took place. John used new ways of relating, learning, and influencing change as the foundation of his leadership.

Facilitating Organizational Learning

In a knowledge era, an intelligent adaptation strategy is to accelerate the shared learning that occurs in an organization. The faster an organization can learn together and apply new insights, the quicker it adapts to changing conditions in the external environment. Therefore, leadership in a networked knowledge era experiments with and focuses on ways organizations and groups continually learn. On an individual level, self-awareness and knowledge are needed to sustain group awareness. As the critical mass of self-aware individuals increases in an organization, the organization's capacity to learn also expands. As organizations model deep learning, they also support and teach individuals to engage in learning as well.

Developing the Capacities of Others

Leadership in organic systems is not the kind of leadership that one person can do. It is leadership that requires many people—a leader-full organization. In an organic system, one person cannot control the system, nor can one person fully understand it. Many people working toward a core purpose all influence the system at large in a common direction. Therefore, models of collaborative, shared, or multi-level leadership become more important and critical in organic organizations. Developing the capacities of others becomes essential in building a leader-full organization.

These five focuses, meaning making, facilitating the flow of energy, organizational renewal, facilitating organizational learning, and developing the capacities of others, form a beginning nucleus for the four new ways of leading, relating, learning, and influencing change. As these four new ways are woven together they become more seamless and at the same time build our awareness of how they relate to and support each other.

Practicing New Ways of Leading

Here is a sampling of strategies for practicing new ways of leading.

1. *Use questions worth asking as strange attractors in the system.* A question worth asking is a well-packed question without a simple answer. It often is a question that reflects the tensions of opposites or presents a paradox. By bringing a worthy question to the staff to reflect on over the course of time, the question creates a subtle adjustment in the staff's approach to their jobs. The question acts like a strange attractor in the system. It is not necessary to answer the question; the existence of the question and continual wrestling with it provide direction without control. Over time, the situation that triggered the initial question may actually be resolved by the individual shifts that have occurred in the way the staff have adjusted their work.

2. *Spend time articulating individual and institutional core values.* The core values of an organization have more power to create alignment than any performance appraisal or goal setting process. By articulating individual core values and seeing how these core values match up to the mission and vision of our institutions, a natural shared meaning evolves. The exercise of making visible individual core values and their relationship to the institution's core values becomes an important way to give the staff confidence to self organize their behavior around their own and the institution's values.

3. *Facilitate learning conversations.* A learning conversation is different than a debate or discussion. It is a shared dialogue where different opinions are seen as an opportunity to gain a greater understanding of what everyone involved is thinking, feeling, and perceiving. Facilitating learning conversations is a key strategy for generating the information and learning needed in this self-reflective process. This notion is not new; however, we are familiar with more traditional language like assessment and formative evaluation. This strategy takes these ideas and extends them into a way of being. Facilitating learning conversations increases the number and ways we formally and informally come together, reflect on what we are doing, what we are accomplishing, and what we are learning collectively.

4. *See and influence fractals.* Taking time to observe fractals that reoccur on different scales throughout the organization is a way to see how the system is organizing itself. Identifying and articulating fractals can increase awareness of pattern formation in an organization. As patterns are named, meaning and responses can be generated.

Moreover, identifying fractals that are antithetical to what we are try-ing to accomplish gives insight to areas that need to change.

5. *Search for patterns.* Often, we spend our days in the trenches work-ing on the multiple tasks we need to get done that day. This behavior is like getting swept up on the dance floor. To gain perspective, we need to step off the dance floor and go up to the balcony to see the emergent patterns that evolve from dynamics of the system. Leading networked, knowledge-based organizations requires us to see pat-terns and help others do the same.

6. *Develop and model a systems perspective.* Each of us may do this dif-ferently. For some, practicing and talking with others who also share this perspective helps make a systems perspective conscious. Others may prefer reading as a way of bringing these concepts into awareness and practice. Awareness is the first stage of modeling a systems per-spective. The second stage involves playing with these concepts in our day-to-day work. The more we understand and practice systems think-ing the more we personally integrate these concepts. This personal integration of a systems perspective is brought to every meeting, con-versation, or problem solving activity in which we are engaged.

7. *Challenge others to see systems.* Once we begin to see things in larg-er patterns, blur our boundaries, and color outside of the lines, our next role is to challenge others to explore systemic perspectives as a way of viewing the organization. When colleagues use a "parts men-tality" in their work, their operating assumptions need to be chal-lenged. Compare the parts mentality with holistic perspectives and see if the dialogue helps both of you see a bigger picture. One vice president bought a book on systems thinking for all the directors in the student affairs division as a staff development tool. Another vice president included a systems thinking session as part of the division's professional development activities.

The new role we propose for student affairs is to *individually practice new ways of leading and apply this knowledge in our departments and our divisions.* We also need to *help institutions practice new ways of leading.* If we are able to accomplish this goal, institutions will be able to respond more effectively to the external challenges that are facing us, and we will be better able to teach our students the capacities needed for their lives. The third section will delineate the new assumptions of working in a networked knowledge era, identify the new roles for insti-tutional change agents, and identify new capacities that are needed to implement the four new ways of working.

Reflective Questions:

1. How can you increase spatial awareness in your work and organization?
2. How can you increase the inter-relational awareness in your work and organization?
3. What emergent variables have you used in your work?
4. What fractals do you see operating in your organization?
5. How do you develop the capacities of others you work with?
6. What are some of the questions worth asking that you could use as a strange attractor in your organization?
7. What does leading from a systemic perspective mean to you?
8. Draw the relationship you see between new ways of leading, learning, changing, and relating.
9. What core values are embedded in your organization?
10. How have you used core values to build cohesion in your organization?

Part Three
Systemic Leadership:
Integrating the Four New
Ways of Working

Chapter 6

Reframing Assumptions and Roles

"In order to learn we must be able to let go of, or modify, outdated beliefs."

—Mark Youngblood

While the traditional hierarchical world still exists, we are experiencing an overlay of a networked knowledge world. As this overlay increases in its power to shape how we function day to day, the network will eventually transcend the hierarchy. Until this time, we will live with operating rules and underlying assumptions that fit both the hierarchy and the network. The purpose of this chapter is to name the underlying beliefs and assumptions of working within a networked knowledge era. We are focusing on these assumptions because we assume most of us know what the assumptions and rules for operating in a hierarchy are since we have grown up in that world. By naming the beliefs and assumptions that have explanatory power for networks, we can more intentionally apply them to our work. However, if you are working in a closed system under controlled conditions, these assumptions will not apply because networks by definition are open and, therefore, uncontrollable systems.

Underlying Assumptions for Working in a Networked Knowledge Era

Each of the new ways of relating, influencing change, learning, and leading has specific underlying assumptions. In this section, we will describe a primary traditional assumption and juxtapose it with the underlying assumptions needed for each new way of working. Then we will identify a new role for student affairs professionals to help their institutions adapt to these external forces.

New Ways of Relating

As stated earlier, a networked world operates on linkages and connections. In order to increase the effectiveness when working in a networked world, we need to optimize these connections. One way to do this is for student affairs practitioners to prioritize their time to build relationships. Professionals, who are effective employees, take time to nurture and maintain their network of relationships within an organization. Intentionally building relationships is a key result of new ways of relating.

Traditional Assumption: The traditional underlying assumption is that relationships in hierarchical organizations are predetermined based on one's position and location in an organization. Additionally, autonomy is highly valued which results in a control orientation toward relationships.

New Assumptions: In a networked world, the underlying assumptions that support new ways of relating are as follows:

• *Never underestimate the interrelatedness that exists within a system.* The traditional view minimizes the number of connections we need to focus on. As networks and connections increase, underestimating interrelatedness becomes a liability. If we underestimated the connections in a networked world, it would be like making decisions with only 10% of the information when actually 100% of the information is available. Ignoring connections actually hinders our capacity to anticipate organizational dynamics.

• *Variables in a system mutually shape each other.* The traditional assumption is that there are few independent variables that can predict many dependent variables. In a networked world, the number of variables in play radically increases due to the openness of the system. When these variables interact they mutually shape one another, causing circles of causality rather than single chains of causality. Networks are too dynamic for linear causality. Since variables mutually shape each other, we need to think relationally in a networked world.

• *Networks facilitate the flow of emotions as well as information.* The traditional assumption is that knowledge and information flows through supervised channels within an organization. In a network, there is no "governing" switch on quality control. The network will amplify misinformation. Powerful emotional reactions, deep wisdom, and mass amounts of data all flow through a system with equity and all will be amplified by the network. In addition, the receivers in the network will determine the reliability and validity of these messages. These multiple receivers will construct their own reality of the message. Therefore, we need to increase our emotional stability, and trust in our relationships, and ourselves to decrease the misinformation and amplification of negative emotions.

The new role for student affairs practitioners is to influence the organization to think and practice new ways of relating. This entails optimizing relationships and connections in the organization and the external environment, thinking and acting relationally, and fostering emotional intelligence.

New Ways of Influencing Change

Networks change differently than traditional hierarchies. Influencing change within a network is affected by the nature of a network. Networks are highly dynamic, and therefore, change is a constant. Because networks are open systems, the number of variables in play also increases, and in turn, increases the level of complexity. Therefore, organic strategies can be more effective in influencing change in a network.

Traditional Assumptions: Traditional assumptions from hierarchical organizations suggest that change is a controlled, incremental event accomplished by the effective application of power and force in the form of positional power and organizational resources. This belief implies that one can control the timing and direction of change with a degree of precision that is not possible in networks. In fact, networks actively resist this approach. Networks respond to intentional influencing, but not to direct applications of force. Nor are they controllable—there are too many variables.

New Assumptions: In a networked world, the underlying assumptions that support new ways of influencing change are as follows:

• *Multiple persons intentionally influencing in the same direction are needed to activate/create change.* The traditional view of change is that one person initiates it and often the person at the top of the organization is given credit. However, in a network, collaboration is both a prerequisite and a requirement for influencing change. These change collaborators must be strategically placed throughout the network and work in concert with each other to nudge the system in a common direction.

• *Non-linear logic is necessary to understand the change dynamics in a network.* In traditional change strategies, there is an assumption that change is a step-by-step process that builds toward a specific goal in a rational and linear way. The dynamics of a network are influenced by variations occurring at a distance, which can result in non-linear jumps in the local context. The network is paradoxical in that it can both accelerate and delay change.

• *Change can be triggered from anywhere.* Traditional assumptions suggest that change can only be initiated from key positions within an organization and must be backed by organizational resources. In networks, change can be initiated from anywhere because the resources that can be used to influence the system are available to everyone in the network. The resources needed to influence change in a networked system are relationships, powerful ideas, shared commitment to a common intent, and access to a communication vehicle.

The new role for student affairs practitioners is to influence change organically in the organization. Individually, this entails an engaged active mindset followed by a systemic perspective that targets the points of leverage within a network. Organizationally, it requires active collaboration directed toward a shared intent. Having others to collaborate with to influence change implies the capacity to build trusting and intentional relationships.

New Ways of Learning

In a networked world, learning is constant. Ongoing learning is how organizations adapt to changing conditions in the external environment. On an individual level, learning integrates knowledge with capacities and practice. Being able to learn from day to day practice or feed insights from skill acquisition into knowledge are ways of increasing "learning access points" to a networked world. For an integrated learner, practice, capacities, and knowledge feed back on each other to accelerate and reinforce changes in thinking and perceiving. On an organizational level, shared learning takes the integrated learning of many individuals and leverages it into a collective organizational intelligence capable of applying these new insights into a higher degree of sustainability for the organization.

Traditional Assumptions: Traditional assumptions suggest that effective leaders can fully understand their organization and the external environment. It also implies that "not knowing" is a liability for positional leaders. However, the complex dynamics of a networked world make it impossible for one person to know and understand the system. The emphasis on organizational shared learning requires diverse perspectives to see the network dynamics and a process that facilitates the generation of shared organizational knowledge.

New Assumptions: In a networked world, the underlying assumptions that support new ways of learning are as follows:

• *What is important to know changes—sometimes drastically.* Because networks are dynamic, they are never stable enough to completely know the system. This means we will never know all we think we need to know in order to make a decision. Rules of what information is important will also change as the network evolves.

• *We can never learn enough or unlearn enough—therefore continual learning and unlearning is critical.* Sometimes network dynamics cause non-linear jumps in the direction or functioning of the network. When this occurs, one of the challenges is to forget the things we have learned that no longer help explain the dynamics of the system.

• *Learning is social—it occurs in concert with others.* Traditionally our school systems have structured learning as an individual activity. In a networked world, individual learning will be, by its nature, limiting. Therefore, learning with others and sharing differences actually facilitates a more holistic understanding of the nature of the networked world.

The new role for student affairs practitioners is to introduce shared learning processes into organizational decision making and planning. This entails bringing our skills of facilitating shared learning in student organizations and residence halls to an institutional level.

New Ways of Leading

A networked world needs new ways of leading. Networks operate like an infinite game; they are not bounded by time or a specific playing field. They continue to operate non-stop and the playing field constantly changes. Therefore, leadership in a networked world continually seeks better ways to adapt to changing conditions and thrive over the long term. Short-term effectiveness is valued in finite games, because if we just put in an extra effort and win the game, the organization will have a breathing space to relax and rejuvenate before the next game. Networks operate over the long term and their survival depends on how well people can pace themselves for endurance rather than a sprint.

Leadership in a networked world concerns itself with the development of human resources that can provide continued leadership over time.

Traditional Assumptions: Traditional hierarchical leadership assumptions suggest that leaders are individuals who hold positions of authority. In the constantly changing networked world, individuals in positions of authority do not have enough power to influence because networks do not have a single lever to pull to start the assembly line of change. Nor do positional leaders have enough information to fully understand the whole system. Leadership in a networked organization can only be understood through a systemic set of actions not the actions of a lone individual.

New Assumptions: In a networked world, the underlying assumptions that support new ways of relating are as follows:

• *Leadership facilitates the process.* Traditional leadership assumptions focus on vision and direction of leadership and sometimes suggest that the means justify the ends. However, in a networked organization, both the process and product are taken into consideration. Due to the connectivity of a network, the way we do things becomes as important as what we do. Paying attention to how we communicate, involving others, building community, and integrating our work are all-important aspects of leadership within a networked world.

• *Networked leadership pays attention to meaning and forces of cohesion.* Traditional hierarchical assumptions assume that policies, procedures, goals, power, and supervisors have ensured control within an organization. Networks do not respond to control strategies; therefore, we need to seek new ways of reinforcing organizational cohesion. The seeking and creation of meaning in our work is one good example. Other intangibles like values and purpose also help sustain organizational cohesion.

• *There are many agents of leadership dispersed throughout a networked organization.* Leadership within a networked world can be practiced from anywhere. In this sense, leadership has the potential of being abundant especially if we think of it as non-positional—not just attached to position and rank. If leadership capacities are encouraged and developed, anyone in the network can become an agent of leadership.

The new role for student affairs practitioners is the development of systemic leadership. Systemic leadership goes beyond new ways of leading to encompass all four new ways of working. This kind of leadership incorporates and weaves the assumptions and practices of new ways of relating, influencing change, learning, and leading into a whole cloth.

In Table 6.1 the relationship between the driving forces of change, new ways of working, underlying assumptions, and the new role for student affairs is summarized.

New Assumptions and New Roles for Student Affairs

Forces of Change	Resulting Underlying Assumptions for New Ways of Working	Student Affairs Role in the Organization
Networked	Relating: • never underestimate the interrelatedness that exists within a system • variables in a system mutually shape each other • networks facilitate the flow of emotions as well as information	Influence the organization to think and practice new ways of relating
Networked	Influencing change: • multiple people intentionally influencing in the same direction are needed to activate / create change • non-linear logic is necessary to understand change dynamics in a network • change can be triggered from anywhere	Influence change organically

Knowledge	Learning: • what is important to know changes—sometimes drastically • we can never learn enough or unlearn enough • learning is social—it occurs in concert with others	Introduce shared learning processes into organizational decision making
Networked and Knowledge	Leading: • leadership facilitates the process • networked leadership pays attention to meaning and forces of cohesion • there are many agents of leadership dispersed throughout a networked organization	Develop systemic leadership

Table 6.1

This chapter outlined the underlying assumptions and the new roles for student affairs professionals within their institutions. The following chapter describes the capacities needed for student affairs practitioners to be effective in their new roles in a networked knowledge era.

Chapter 7

Capacities for a Networked Knowledge World

"The real discovery consists not in finding new lands, but in seeing with new eyes."

—Marcel Proust

The title of our book is *Systemic Leadership: Enriching the Meaning of our Work.* We chose this title to name a new form of leadership that meets the demands of two external driving forces of our world—networks and knowledge. Systemic leadership actively incorporates, integrates, and practices the four new ways of working—relating, influencing change, learning, and leading. It is a higher order of leadership, one that matches the complexity of the system in which we are and will continue to work. The four new ways of working each lead to new roles for student affairs practitioners. These roles require the refinement of some traditional skills that student affairs professionals have practiced and the development of new capacities.

A capacity is defined as the ability to absorb new knowledge or skills and be able to do something with them. This definition brings together into an effective relationship the unique roles that knowledge, skills, and practice play in integrating our learning. In this chapter we will identify eleven new capacities that flow from the four new ways of working. Each of these capacities has a personal and a systemic leadership application. It is assumed that individuals seeking to increase their capacities for systemic leadership will understand that personal transformation is connected to, and necessary for, developing the capacities for systemic leadership.

The relationship between the individual and the organizational leadership capacities looks like a double helix in a DNA strand. One strand of the capacities is related to self-development, while the other strand is related to the capacities of organizational leadership. These two strands intertwine to create an operating code that informs our behavior as we apply these new ways of working. The self-development strand has relationships to other individual capacities. Similarly, the organizational leadership strand has relationships with other organizational leadership capacities. The double helix metaphor implies that both strands are also in relationship with and to each other. In other words, the capacities of the self and the organizational capacities mutually shape each other and together create systemic leadership. The interrelationship between and among self and system capacities together creates a holistic template for our intentional professional development.

Capacities for a Networked Knowledge Era

There are eleven new capacities that complement the new ways of working in a networked knowledge era. Each of the eleven capacities has an individual and an organizational application. This section will identify these capacities and the relationship of each to the new ways of working.

Active Engagement

Active engagement is one of the capacities necessary for influencing change on both an individual and organizational level. On an individual level, the capacity of active engagement involves *developing the mindset of action*. We all make choices of how we engage in our organizations. Will we be withdrawn, cynical, disenfranchised, a feigned participant, a victim? Or will we be actively engaged, a committed participant, a leader, an active change agent? Networks are shaped through the actions of participants in the network. Therefore, an individual capacity in a networked world is to bring a mindset of action instead of passivity to our work. A person can influence a network from anywhere within the system—but only if by acting.

On an organizational level, active engagement is demonstrated when one *engages in purposeful influencing*. This is the organizational leadership capacity that flows from active engagement. On an individual level, a person believes that actions can make a difference and therefore chooses action over passivity. On an organizational level, individuals take this action orientation and learn how to intentionally influence the system. This requires individuals to learn how the system operates, what their role within the system is, who can influence change, and where the leverage points are within the system that allow natural dynamics to bring about transformation.

Collaboration

The capacity of collaboration facilitates two new ways of working. On an individual level, it contributes to new ways of relating. The organizational variation of collaboration contributes to new ways of influencing change. On an individual level, the capacity of collaboration requires *the development of trusting and trustworthy relationships formed in the context of authenticity*. This capacity operates on the personal level but is a necessary prerequisite for the collaboration that is needed for the systemic capacity of influencing change in a networked organization. When we trust others, we share our thoughts and feelings because we believe what we say will not be held against us. When others share their thoughts and feelings with us, they perceive us to be trustworthy—and we will not hold their thoughts against them. If we have relationships built on trust we will be more open and able to collaborate with others. In addition, if we are authentic with others, we bring into our relationships the capability to disagree with respect. Authenticity is necessary for individual relationships and is also a prerequisite for collaboration on a systemic level.

On an organizational level, this capacity involves *cultivating collaborative relationships*. This is the organizational leadership capacity that relates to influencing change. It is supported by the capacity of developing trusting, trustworthy, and authentic relationships. If this capacity is practiced and the mindset of action and purposeful influencing is present, the next capacity that is needed to influence change is creating a network of individuals who will help influence the system in a desired direction (Kotter, 1996). Collaboration is absolutely necessary to the change process in a networked system.

Continual Learning

The capacity of continual learning supports new ways of learning on both the individual and organizational level. On an individual level, this capacity involves becoming an integrated learner. An *integrated learner* continues to create feedback loops between the domains of knowledge, development of new skills, and daily practice in order to accelerate and inform learning and insights. Each domain is an important lens to access what is happening in the dynamically changing network.

Individual integrated learning is necessary for facilitating shared learning on an organizational level.

Facilitating shared learning is the organizational leadership capacity needed for continual learning. It is not enough in a networked world to be an active individual learner. Due to the constant change, groups and organizations need to accelerate the amount of shared knowledge, insights, and learning they acquire so they can adapt to the changing conditions of their environment. The purpose of continual learning is to adapt to the external environment and thereby survive and thrive. Facilitating shared learning processes becomes an important capacity for the learning organization.

Diversify Perspectives

The capacity of diversifying perspectives contributes to two different ways of working. On the individual level, it is necessary for new ways of relating. The organizational application of leveraging multiple perspectives is necessary for new ways of learning. *Thriving on diversity* is the personal capacity that supports the organizational capacity of using multiple perspectives to generate shared knowledge. Appreciating different perspectives—a requirement for full understanding of a networked system, has to start with our individual responses to diversity. Do we value and respect difference? Do we believe that diversity enhances and enriches our personal lives? Individuals who thrive on diversity would seek it out and actively incorporate different perspectives, experiences, and individuals into their lives and worldview.

Leveraging multiple perspectives is the organizational leadership capacity needed for diversifying perspectives. A network has a diverse number of viewpoints, all of which are necessary to understand the whole. As individuals thrive on diversity, organizational learning requires different perspectives to more fully understand a network. New ways of learning seek out and leverage multiple perspectives to facilitate the shift from individual intelligence to collective wisdom.

Emotional Competence

The capacity of emotional competence contributes to new ways of relating on both the individual and organizational level. *Developing the capacity to be mindful of and empathize with others* is the individual application of emotional competence. We can sleepwalk through life, but it will not help us to live effectively in the 21st Century. The capacity of being mindful means that we pay attention to what is happening around us. Mindfulness calls us to live in the present. Many times we have emotional memories that interfere with and hijack our perceptions of the present. When we are mindful, we are aware of actions, our reactions, and ourselves. Over time, this awareness allows us to make active choices of how we behave that helps us build and maintain relationships based on trust and authenticity. Having empathy with others applies personal mindfulness to being present for another individual. Empathy and mindfulness are necessary for the practice of individual emotional competence. They are also prerequisites for facilitating organizational emotional competence.

Facilitating the development of organizational emotional competence is the organizational variation of this capacity. In a networked world, emotions flow freely through the connections. An organization can be swamped with emotional overload. This capacity applies individual mindfulness and empathy at the group and organizational level. When groups and organizations increase their collective emotional awareness, they bring more conscious choice into their relationships with each other. They can choose to be more present, to not blame, to not judge or exclude others. They are able to work through difficult situations without hurting their relationships and as a result their individual and collective learning is accelerated.

Engage with Paradox

Embracing paradoxes is the individual capacity needed for new ways of learning in a networked world. Networks are non-linear in nature. They do not follow the logical, rational thinking processes we have learned and value. Paradoxes often provide a way of seeing the non-linear nature of networks. Seeking out paradoxes and living with them can prepare us for the jumps and leaps that are natural dynamics in a networked system. Embracing paradoxes is an antidote for either-or thinking. Paradoxes invite us to live with polar opposites in peaceful co-existence.

Optimizing tensions to facilitate organizational learning is needed for practicing the capacity of engaging paradox in systemic leadership (Heifetz, 1994). Optimizing the relationship between opposites can help systems evolve. For example, the tension between chaos and control can lead to new forms of innovation in an organization. Optimizing the tension between challenge and support can facilitate growth and development in students. The tension between anxiety and boredom can facilitate learning. Effectiveness comes from optimizing efficiency and redundancy. Systemic leadership optimizes the tensions between opposites as a way to accelerate shared learning on an individual and organizational level.

Meaning Making

The capacity of meaning making contributes to new ways of leading on both the individual and organizational level. *Actively seeking meaning in your personal life and work* is the individual level capacity of meaning making. The search for meaning has been a human pastime for centuries—some would say that this is the spiritual nature of human beings. A networked world invites a search for meaning. Given the many variables in play, grasping the meaning of the relationships among them is a requirement for making connections between ones work and what one intends to actively shape.

Fostering communities of meaning in organizations is the organizational leadership capacity of meaning making and is related to new ways of leading. On a leadership level, fostering communities that are organized around a shared sense of significance is a new way of fostering cohesion and unity in a networked organization. Communities of meaning in a networked world can be created over great distances. For example, a network of practitioners all working toward the transformation of higher education can form a loosely connected but powerful force for change. Systemic leadership helps name the meaning that in turn facilitates the creation of a community of shared significance—even if it is at a distance.

Paradigm Cognition

Understanding the power of context is the individual level capacity of paradigm cognition and contributes to new ways of leading. A necessary capacity of a networked world is to recognize the paradigm that provides the most powerful explanation of the dynamics of the system. One of the critical aspects to paradigm recognition is the awareness and understanding of the local context. The local context in a networked system is a powerful shaper of system dynamics. The individual capacity is to recognize context as an important variable and work to understand it and its effect on possible interventions when influencing the system.

Pattern recognition is the organizational leadership capacity of paradigm cognition needed in new ways of leading (Keidel, 1995). In any situation there are multiple assumptions and paradigms that can be chosen to provide explanations that increase our effectiveness at work. If a closed system is operating, traditional assumptions and paradigms have more power to explain the expected dynamics. Being able to recognize when different paradigms are most useful is a needed capacity for systemic leading.

Profound Change

Profound change is the capacity that contributes to new ways of influencing change on both personal and organizational levels (Quinn, 1996). *Personal transformation* is the individual capacity needed for the facilitation of deep organizational change. Most people will not change if the opinion leaders of an organization are not willing to do what they are asking of others. Any influencing relationship is a two way street. If we are asking others to change, we must also be willing to be influenced by them.

Organizational transformation is the organizational leadership capacity related to deep change. Transformation of an organization is influenced and shaped by the transformation of individuals within the organization. In turn, individuals are influenced and shaped by profound change in an organization. As we work on our own transformation we can also influence profound change in a network.

Systems Cognition

Systems cognition is a capacity that is necessary for new ways of learning on both individual and organizational levels. *Seeing connections* within a system or network is the individual level capacity of systems cognition. Networks thrive on connections, so seeing connections is essential. Being able to see the system in which we practice is a capacity for new ways of leading. Individuals can become "systems thinkers" when they see how their "part of the organization" fits with the whole system, when they see how the past effects the present, how the present effects the future, and when they can see the relationships and processes that affect the dynamics of an organization. Each of these connections, once seen, increases the effectiveness we have in our work in a networked system.

Applying system dynamics to leadership practice is the organizational leadership capacity of systems cognition. Once individuals can see systems, they need to apply this knowledge to the organizational level by developing the capacity to leverage the dynamics of the network to facilitate and influence change. Systems operate as more than the sum of their parts. System dynamics looks at how the whole organization behaves, anticipates, understands, and then actively influences change.

Sustainability

Sustaining your personal balance is the individual level of the capacity of sustainability and is necessary for new ways of leading. Because networks constantly change and never shut down, we need to develop and conserve our energy and resources over the long haul. In finite games, we can come close to burn out or injury because we know there will be a rest period between games. In a network there is no rest period—the action is non-stop. Therefore, we need to develop the capacity for sustaining our own balance so we can maintain endurance over time.

Maintaining an orientation of *stewardship over time* toward human, other living, and material resources is the organizational leadership capacity of sustainability which supports new ways of leading. On an individual level we need to develop the capacity for balance. The organizational application is to develop the capacity for sustaining the organization and its resources for the long term. This brings the value of stewardship to systemic leadership.

These eleven capacities are summarized in Table 7.1. The table orders them by the capacity and the individual and organizational leadership application. It also connects the capacity and their sub-sets to each new way of working.

Capacities for New Ways of Relating, Influencing Change, Learning, and Leading

Capacity	Individual Capacity and Organizational Leadership	Relationship to New Ways of Working
Active engagement	Self: a mind set of action Organizational: purposeful influencing	Influencing change Influencing change
Collaboration	Self: trusting, trustworthy, and authenticity Organizational: cultivating collaborative relationships	Relating Influencing change

Continual learning	Self: integrated learning Organizational: facilitating shared learning	Learning Learning
Diversify perspectives	Self: thrive on diversity Organizational: leveraging multiple perspectives	Relating Learning
Emotional competence	Self: empathy and mindfulness Organizational: facilitate organizational emotional competence.	Relating Relating
Engage paradox	Self: embrace paradox Organizational: optimizing tensions	Learning Learning
Meaning making	Self: meaning making Organizational: fostering communities of meaning	Leading Leading
Paradigm cognition	Self: understanding context Organizational: pattern recognition	Leading Leading
Profound change	Self: personal transformation Organizational: organizational transformation	Influencing change Influencing change
Systems cognition	Self: seeing connections Organizational: apply system dynamics to leadership	Leading Leading
Sustainability	Self: balance Organizational: stewardship over time	Leading Leading

Table 7.1

Systemic leadership integrates and incorporates new ways of relating, influencing change, learning, and leading. When we engage in systemic leadership, we use each of the new ways of doing things in concert with each other to create a seamless approach to the practice of leadership. The four new ways of working support and enhance each other.

Enriching the Meaning of Our Work: Putting it All Together

In higher education, student affairs professionals have aspects of many capacities needed for the practice of systemic leadership. Chapter Six summarized the underlying assumptions of new ways of working and identified new roles for student affairs practitioners who choose to become systemic leaders. This chapter described the personal and organizational capacities necessary to practice systemic leadership. The following table integrates these assumptions and roles with the new capacities introduced in this chapter. (See Table 7.2)

New Ways *involve*	Reframing Assumptions *for our*	New Roles *and the*	Capacities *to be effective in our roles.*
Relating	• Never underestimate the interrelatedness that exists within a system. • Variables in a system mutually shape each other. • Networks facilitate the flow of emotions and information.	Influence the organization to think and practice new ways of relating.	COLLABORATION · EMOTIONAL COMPETENCE · DIVERSIFY PERSPECTIVE
Influencing Change	• Multiple people intentionally influencing in the same direction are needed to activate/create change. • No linear logic is necessary to understand the change dynamics in a network. • Change can be triggered from anywhere.	Influence change organically in the organization.	PROFOUND CHANGE · ACTIVE ENGAGEMENT
Learning	• What is important to know changes—sometimes drastically. • We can never learn enough or unlearn enough—therefore continual learning and unlearning is critical. • Learning is social—it occurs in concert with others.	Introduce shared learning processes into organizational decision making and planning.	ENGAGE PARADOX · CONTINUAL LEARNING
Leading	• Leadership facilitates the process. • Networked leadership pays attention to meaning and forces of cohesion. • There are many agents of leadership dispersed throughout a networked organization.	Development of systemic leadership.	SUSTAINABILITY · SYSTEMS COGNITION · PARADIGM COGNITION · MEANING MAKING

LEGEND: ORGANIZATIONAL CAPACITIES ▢　INDIVIDUAL CAPACITIES ▢

Table 7.2

Summary

This book describes two major forces of change in the world and it makes a case for the practice of a new approach to leadership—systemic leadership—to respond to these forces. Each of the four new ways of working responds to the two powerful forces of the networked knowledge era. As we combine the four new ways of working and integrate them seamlessly into one practice of leadership, we create a systemic approach to leadership. The practice of systemic leadership challenges us to formulate new assumptions that explain our world and organizations. Applying these assumptions to our work leads us to adopt new roles within our organizations. These new roles can be practiced from anywhere, not just through positions of authority. The development and refinement of the eleven individual and organizational capacities are necessary for the practice of systemic leadership and the performance of our new roles within the academy. With these capacities and a systemic leadership perspective, we can help higher education transform itself and prepare students to work in a networked knowledge era.

We believe we need to dramatically transform our organizations. This book has provided a vision, new roles, and capacities to help accomplish this important task. The time is short but the possibilities for accelerated change increase in a networked world. However, we need to start now. We believe that student affairs practitioners can play a special role in the transformation of higher education. It is time for student affairs professionals to bring their perspectives, skills, and capacities to help the transformation of our institutions and increase their capacity to respond to a networked knowledge world.

The ideas in this book introduce four new ways of working. While the themes provide an integrated whole, they are not complete until practitioners experiment with them. It is through the practice of these new ways of working that the ideas in this book come alive. We invite the reader to embark on a journey toward systemic leadership. We leave you with this quote from Dee Hock (1996):

"If not this, what? If not now, when? If not you, who?"

References

Allen, K., & Cherrey, C. (1994). Shifting paradigms and practices in student affairs. In J. Fried (Ed.) *Different voices:Gender and Perspective in Student Affairs Administration.* National Association for Student Personnel Administrators Monograph, 16, 1-29.

Allen, K., & Garb, E. (1993). Reinventing student affairs: Something old and something new. *National Association of Student Personnel Administrators Journal, 30*(2), 10-20.

Allen, K. E., Stelzner, S. P., & Wielkiewicz, R. M. (1998). The ecology of leadership: Adapting to the challenges of a changing world. *The Journal of Leadership Studies, 5*(2), 62-82.

Astin, H., Astin, A., et al. (1996). *A social change model of leadership and development Version III.* Higher Education Research Institute of California, Los Angeles.

Banathy, B.H. (1993). The cognitive mapping of societal systems: Implications for education. In Laszlo, E.& Masulli I. (Eds.) *The evolution of cognitive maps: New paradigms for the twenty-first century.* Amsterdam: Gordon and Breach Science Publishers S.A.

Barr, R., & Tagg, J. (1995). From teaching to learning—A new paradigm for undergraduate education. *Change, 27*(6), 13-25.

Bateson, M.C. (1994). *Peripheral vision.* San Francisco: Berrett-Koehler.

Bennis, W., Parikh, J., Lessen, R. (1994). *Beyond leadership: Balancing economics, ethics and ecology.* Cambridge: Blackwell.

Bolman, L.G., & Deal, T.E. (1984). *Modern approaches to understanding and managing organizations.* San Francisco: Jossey-Bass.

Capra, F. (1996). *The web of life.* New York: Anchor Books Doubleday.

Capra, F. (1992). Changes in management–management of change: The systematic approach. *World Business Academy Perspectives, 6*(3).

Cherrey, C., & Isgar, R. (1998). Leadership education in the context of the new millennium. *Concepts & connections–The future of leadership education.* College Park, MD: NCLP.

Clark, D. (1985). Emerging Paradigms in Organizational Theory and Research. In Y.S. Lincoln (Ed.); *Organizational Theory and Inquiry: The Paradigm Revolution,* (pp. 43-78). Beverly Hills: Sage.

Conner, D. (1995). *Managing at the speed of change.* New York: Villard Books.

de Geus, A. (1997) *The living company: Habits for survival in a turbulent business environment.* Boston: Harvard Business School Press.

Dörner, D. (1996). *The logic of failure: Why things go wrong and what can we do to make them right.* New York: Metropolitan Books.

Duderstadt, J. (1995). *Academic renewal at Michigan: Executive strategies.* In S. Massey (Ed.); Stanford Forum for Higher Education Futures.

Duderstadt, J. (1997, July). Revolutionary changes: Understanding the challenges and the possibilities. *NACUBO Business Officer, 1,* 1-18.

Eoyang, G.H. (1997). *Coping with chaos: Seven simple tools.* Cheyenne: Lagumo Corp.

Eoyang, G.H. (1993, Sept.). *Questions and answers about chaos in organizations.* Paper presented at the Chaos and Leadership conference, Minneapolis, MN.

Gleick, J. (1987). *Chaos: Making a new science.* New York: Penguin Books.

Goleman, D. (1998). *Emotional intelligence.* New York: Bantam Books.

Goleman, D. (1997). *Working with emotional intelligence.* New York: Bantam Books.

Halal, N. (1998). *The infinite resource: Creating and leading the knowledge enterprise.* San Francisco: Jossey-Bass.

Hammer, M., & Champy, J. (1993). *Reengineering the corporation: A manifesto for business revolution.* New York: Harper Collins Publishers.

Handy, C. (1989). *The age of unreason.* Boston: Harvard Business School Press.

Heenan, D.A. & Bennis, W. (1999). *Co-leaders: The power of great partnerships.* New York: John Wiley & Sons, Inc.

Helgesen, S. (1995). *The web of inclusion.* New York: Doubleday.

Heifetz, R. (1994). *Leadership without easy answers.* Cambridge: Belknap Press of Harvard University Press.

Hock, D. W. (1996, October). *System thinking.* Keynote address presented at the Systems Thinking Conference. San Francisco.

Hoffer, E. (1973). *Reflections on the human condition.* New York: Harper & Row.

Ikenberry, S. O. (1996). ACE's new president: The challenge is change. *Education Record, 77*(4), 7-13.

Johnson Foundation (1993). An American imperative: Higher expectations for higher education. *Report of the Wingspread Group on Higher Education.* Racine, WI: author.Keidel, R. (1995). *Seeing organizational patterns.* San Francisco: Berrett-Koehler.

Keidel, R. (1995). *Seeing organizational patterns.* San Francisco: Berrett-Koehler.

Kotter, J. (1996) *Leading change.* Boston: Harvard Business School Press.

Kuh, G. (1996). Guiding principles for creating seamless learning environments for undergraduates. *Journal of College Student Development, 37,* 135-148.

Kuh, G., Whitt, E., & Shedd, J. (1987). Student affairs, 2001: A paradigmatic odyssey. *American College Personnel Association Monograph.*

Kuh, G., Douglas, K., Lund, J., Ramir-Gyurnek, J. (1984). *Student learning outside the classroom: Transcending artificial boundaries.* American Journal of Higher Education: Eric Higher Education Report, 8.

Lynch, D., & Kordis, P. (1988). *Strategy of the dolphin: Scoring a win in a chaotic world.* New York: William Morrow and Company, Inc.

Marshall, P., & Wel, C. (1996). The shift to participation. In W. Harman and M. Porter (Eds.) *The new business of business.* San Francisco: Berrett-Koehler.

Matusak, L. (1997). *Finding your voice: Learning to lead anywhere you want to make a difference.* San Francisco: Jossey-Bass.

Morgan, G. (1997). *Imagination: New mindset for seeing, organizing and managing.* San Francisco: Berrett-Koehler.

Negroponte, N. (1995). *Being digital.* New York: Knopf.

Oshry, B. (1995). *Seeing systems: Unblocking the mysteries of organizational life.* San Francisco: Berrett-Koehler.

Quinn, R. (1996). *Deep change: Discovering the leader within.* San Francisco: Jossey-Bass.

Russell, P. (1992). *The white hole in time.* Novato: Origin Press.

Senge, P. (1996). Learning organizations: The promise and the possibilities. *The Systems Thinker, 7*(9).

Senge, P., Kleiner, A., Rovarts, C., Ross, R. & Smith, B. (1994). *The fifth discipline fieldbook: Strategies and tools for building a learning organization.* New York: Doubleday.

Senge, P. (1990). *The fifth discipline: The art and practice of the learning organization.* New York: Currency-Doubleday.

Skinner, B. F. (1953). *Science and human behavior.* New York: Free Press.

Stacey, R. (1992). *Managing the unknowable: Strategic boundaries between order and chaos in organizations*. San Francisco: Jossey-Bass.

Taylor, F. (1915). *The principles of scientific management*. New York: Harper Brothers Publishers.

Taylor, J., & Wacker, W. (1997). *The 500-year delta: What happens after what comes next*. New York: Harper Business.

The net's loss: The flexible, consensual structure Jon Postel helped bring to the internet deserves to continue after his death (1998, Oct. 20). *Financial Times* (London).

The student personnel point of view (1989). *National Association of Student Personnel Administrators Journal*.

The student learning imperative: Implications for student affairs. (1994). Washington, DC: *American College Personnel Association*.

Vaill, P. (1996). *Learning as a way of being*. San Francisco: Jossey-Bass.

Wheately, M. (1995). *Lesson from the new workplace*. CRM Filme.

Wheately, M. (1992). *Leadership in the new science: Learning about organization from an orderly universe*. San Francisco: Berrett-Koehler.

Wheately, M., & Kellner-Rogers, M. (1996). *A simpler way*. San Francisco: Berrett-Koehler.

Youngblood, M. (1997). *Life at the edge of chaos: Creating the quantum organization*. Dallas: Perceval Publishers.

Zohar, D. (1997). *Rewiring the corporate brain: Using the new science to rethink how we structure and lead organizations*. San Francisco: Berrett-Koehler.

Index